D0909427

31-18

The Infante Dom Henrique

(from the Zurara *Chronicle* in the Museu Nacional de Arte Antiga, Lisboa)

Four Centuries of Portuguese Expansion, 1415-1825:

A Succinct Survey

By
C. R. BOXER

UNIVERSITY OF CALIFORNIA PRESS
Berkeley and Los Angeles
and
WITWATERSRAND UNIVERSITY PRESS
Johannesburg
1969

SHENANDOAH COLLEGE
LIBRARY
WINCHESTER, VA.

First Published by the
Witwatersrand University Press
1961
California Reprint, 1969

© 1961 by the Witwatersrand University Press
Standard Book Number 520-01419-7
Library of Congress Catalog Card Number: 74-92672

```
JV      Boxer, C. R.
4211
.B68    Four centuries of
1969    Portuguese expansion,
        1415-1825
325.3469 B69f
```

23410

Printed in the United States of America

CONTENTS

PLATES

MAP

PREFACE

The following pages contain the text of a series of four public lectures delivered by me as Visiting Professor at the Ernest Oppenheimer Institute of Portuguese Studies, University of the Witwatersrand, Johannesburg, in the months of May and June, 1960. I thought that this subject would be appropriate in the year during which the Portuguese are commemorating the 500th anniversary of the death of the Infante Dom Henrique (13 November 1460) and the overseas expansion of Europe which began in his day and generation. I also had in mind the series of lectures given by the first Visiting Professor at the Oppenheimer Institute, Father António da Silva Rego, published under the title of *Portuguese colonization in the sixteenth century: a study of the royal ordinances* (Witwatersrand University Press, 1957). My distinguished predecessor's aim was, in his own words:

> to gather from these remote royal ordinances, lessons regarding human relations between the Portuguese on the one side and Indians, Africans and Brazilians on the other.

In my own series, I have dwelt less on the policies adumbrated at Lisbon than on what actually happened overseas. These lectures therefore survey the history of Portuguese colonization from another standpoint.

It is obvious that in attempting to deal in four hours with a subject that ranges over four centuries in time and four continents in space, I had to be either severely selective or else completely superficial. I trust that I have erred in the former rather than in the latter sense, but nobody is more conscious than myself of how much has been left unsaid.

My sincere thanks are due to the Principal of the University of the Witwatersrand and to the other members of the Board of Portuguese Studies for inviting me to give these lectures in the first place; for sponsoring their publication in this series; and for making my stay in the Union of South Africa so enjoyable. It is, perhaps, hardly necessary to add that the views expressed in these lectures are mine alone. They are published exactly as they were delivered, but the opportunity has been taken to document my assertions by the inclusion of footnotes.

22 July 1960   C. R. BOXER

I

FROM THE MAGHREB TO THE MOLUCCAS,
1415–1521

A sixteenth-century Spanish historian, Francisco López de Gómara, described the Iberian seafarers' discovery of the Ocean route to the East and West Indies as being:

the greatest event since the creation of the world, apart from the incarnation and death of him who created it.[1]

Even nowadays many people, including those who are not Christians, may think that he was not far wrong. For the most striking feature of the history of civilization prior to the Portuguese and Spanish voyages of discovery was the dispersion and isolation of the different branches of mankind. The human societies that waxed and waned in the whole of America, and in a great part of Africa and of the Pacific, were completely unknown to those in Europe and Asia. Western Europe had only the most tenuous and fragmentary knowledge of the great Asian and North African civilizations. These on their side knew little or nothing of Europe and of Africa south of the Sudan—a "dark continent" to them as well as to us—and nothing at all of America. It was the Portuguese pioneers and the Castilian *conquistadores* from the western rim of Christendom who brought together, for better or for worse, the widely sundered branches of the great human family. They thus first made humanity conscious, however dimly, of its essential unity.

[1] ". . . la mayor cosa después de la creación del mundo, sacando la encarnación y muerte del que lo criá". Francisco López de Gómara, *Primera y segunda parte de la historia general de las Indias* (Çaragoça, 1553), Vol. I, p. 4.

Plate 1   **Hottentots of the Cape of Good Hope**

(from an Indo-Portuguese drawing of *c.* 1540 in the Bibl. Casanatense, Rome, Cod. 1889, by courtesy of Padre G. Schurhammer S.J.)

2

We are often told that the peoples of the Iberian peninsula —and particularly the Portuguese—were peculiarly fitted to inaugurate the series of maritime and geographical discoveries which changed the course of world history in the fifteenth and sixteenth centuries. Among their assets in this connection are commonly listed their geographical position in Europe's most advanced window on the Atlantic, and certain racial characteristics evolved in eight centuries of struggle with the Moors. The long Moorish domination in the Peninsula had accustomed many of the Christian inhabitants to regard the swarthier Moor or Arab as a social superior, and the brown Moorish woman as an enviable type of beauty and sexual attractiveness. This last trait is still evinced by the popularity of the folk-tales of the *Moura Encantada*, or enchanted Moorish princess, among the illiterate Portuguese peasantry. From this, it is alleged, it was but a short step to tolerating half-breeds and mixed bloods. Hence the tendency of the Portuguese—and to a lesser degree of the Spaniards—to dispense with the colour-bar. The centuries during which Christian and Muslim struggled for the mastery of the Iberian peninsula were not (we are reminded) epochs of unremitting intolerance and strife. *El Cid Campeador* changed sides more than once; and there was a period in the thirteenth century when Christian, Muslim, and Jewish rites were amicably celebrated in the same temple—the Mosque of Santa María la Blanca at Toledo.[2]

There is obviously some substance in these arguments, but they must not be pushed too far. In the first place, many, perhaps a majority, of the 'Moors' who occupied

[2] The protagonist of this viewpoint is Gilberto Freyre, who has elaborated the theme in his well-known works, *Brazil: an interpretation* (New York, 1945); *Casa Grande e Senzala* (Rio de Janeiro, 1943), 2 vols., this last available in an English translation by Samuel Putnam, *The Masters and the Slaves* (New York, 1946), cf. also Roy Nash, *The Conquest of Brazil* (New York, 1926).

the Iberian peninsula for so long were no darker than the Portuguese, since they were Berbers and not Arabs, nor 'Blackamoors'. Secondly, even if the bitter struggle for the hegemony of the peninsula was punctuated by spells of mutual tolerance, these respites did not last long. The years when the three rival cults were celebrated on an equal footing at Toledo had no more permanent result than had the fleeting Christian-Muslim *rapprochement* achieved in Sicily under the rule of Frederick II, "Stupor Mundi", in the same period. In the fifteenth century, at any rate, the average Iberian Christian—like any other—never referred to the Muslim and the Jewish faiths without adding some injurious epithet. Hatred and intolerance, not sympathy and understanding, for alien creeds and races was the general rule. 'Moors' (i.e. Muslims), Jews, and Gentiles, were alike regarded as doomed to hell fire in the next world. Consequently, they were not likely to be treated with much consideration in this one.

The intolerance was not, of course, only on one side. The Christian crusade had its counterpart in the Muslim *jihad*, or holy war against the unbeliever. The orthodox Muslim regarded with horror all those who would "give associates to God"; and this was just what the Christians did with their Trinity, their Virgin Mary, and (to some extent) with their saints.

Medieval Europe was a harsh and rugged school, and the softer graces of civilization were not more widely cultivated in Portugal than elsewhere. A turbulent and treacherous nobility and gentry; an ignorant and lax clergy; doltish if hard-working peasants and fishermen; and a town rabble of artisans and day-labourers like the Lisbon mob described by Eça de Queiroz five centuries later, "fanatical, filthy, and ferocious"[3]—these constituted the

---

[3] ". . . essa plebe beata, suja e feroz" (Eça de Queiroz, *Os Maias*, Vol. I, p. 1).

social classes from which the pioneer discoverers and colonizers were drawn. Anyone who doubts this need only read the graphic pages of Fernão Lopes, "the best chronicler of any age or nation", as Robert Southey described him.[4]

The first stage of the overseas expansion of Europe can be regarded as beginning with the capture of Ceuta by the Portuguese in 1415 and culminating in the circumnavigation of the world by the Spanish ship *Victoria* in 1519–22. The Portuguese and Spaniards had their precursors in the conquest of the Atlantic Ocean, but the efforts of these adventurers had not changed the course of world history. Vikings had voyaged to North America in the early Middle Ages, but the last of their isolated settlements on Greenland had succumbed to the rigours of the weather and the attacks of the Eskimo before the end of the fifteenth century. Italian and Catalan galleys from the Mediterranean had boldly ventured into the Atlantic on voyages of discovery in the late thirteenth and early fourteenth centuries; but what they sought is uncertain, and what they found is equally obscure, though they may have sighted the Açores. Why did the Iberians succeed where their Mediterranean predecessors had failed; and why did Portugal take the lead when the Biscayan seamen were as enterprising and their ships as good as any in Europe?

Historians are still far from agreed on the precise answers to these questions, but the main impulses behind what is known as the "Age of Discovery" evidently came from a mixture of religious, economic, strategic and political factors. These were by no means always mixed in the same proportions; and motives inspired by Mammon were often inextricably blended with things pertaining to Caesar and to God. At the risk of over-simplification, it may, perhaps,

---

[4] Fernão Lopes, *Crónica de D. João I*, ed. A. Sergio (Porto, 1945-49), 2 vols. Vol. 1, pp. 24-30, 86, 89-92; Vol. 2, pp. 58-59, 64, 243, for some typical instances of medieval savagery. Cf. also *Studia. Revista Semestral*, Vol. 5, p. 167, 1960.

be said that the four main motives which inspired the Portuguese were, in chronological order, (i) crusading zeal, (ii) desire for Guinea gold, (iii) the quest for Prester John, and (iv) the search for spices. An important contributory factor was that during the whole of the fifteenth century Portugal was a united kingdom, virtually free of civil strife; whereas France was distracted by the closing stages of the Hundred Years War—1415 was the date of the battle of Agincourt as well as of the capture of Ceuta and by rivalry with Burgundy; England by the struggle with France and the Wars of the Roses; and Spain and Italy by dynastic and other internal convulsions.

The seizure of Ceuta in 1415, and, more important, its retention, were probably inspired mainly by crusading ardour to deal a blow at the Infidel, and by the desire of the half-English princes of Portugal to be dubbed knights on the field of battle in a spectacular manner. Economic and strategic motives may also have played a part, since Ceuta was both a thriving commercial centre and a bridgehead for an invasion across the straits of Gibraltar. It has been suggested that the fertile corn-growing regions in the hinterland also formed an attraction for the Portuguese, whose own country was even then normally deficient in cereals. Ceuta was one of the terminal ports for the trans-Sahara gold-trade, though how far the Portuguese realized this fact before their capture of the city is uncertain. But the occupation of Ceuta undoubtedly enabled the Portuguese to obtain some information about the Negro lands of the Upper Niger and Senegal river regions where the gold came from. They soon began to realize that they might, perhaps, establish contact with those lands by sea, and so divert the gold-trade from the "caravans of the old Sahara" and the Muslim middlemen of Barbary.[5] They had the more

[5] E. W. Bovill, *Caravans of the old Sahara* (London, 1933), and *The golden trade of the Moors* (London, 1958).

6

incentive to do this, since Western Europe in general and Portugal in particular were then suffering from a serious shortage of precious metals. This was partly due to the drain of silver and gold to the East, to pay for spices and other Oriental imports, and partly to a fall in the production of the central European mines.

The crusading impulse and the search for Guinea gold were soon reinforced by the quest for Prester John. This mythical potentate was vaguely located in "the Indies"—an elastic and shifting term often embracing Ethiopia and East Africa as well as what little was known of Asia. The passage of time, romantic travellers' tales—of which Marco Polo's supply the classic example—and wishful thinking, all combined to build up the late medieval belief that Prester John was a mighty if probably schismatical Christian priest-king. His domains were believed to lie somewhere in the rear of the Islamic powers which occupied a wide belt of territory from Morocco to the Black Sea, thus cutting off Christendom from direct contact with the peoples of Asia and the isolated Coptic Christian kingdom of Abyssinia. From 1402 onwards, occasional Abyssinian monks and envoys reached Europe, and at least one of them got as far as Lisbon in 1452; but the Portuguese still had only a hazy idea of what or where his country was.

This mixed motivation of the Portuguese overseas expansion was explicitly recognized in the Papal Bull *Romanus Pontifex* (8 January 1455), which categorically commended the crusading inspiration of the Infante Dom Henrique and his desire to reach the mysterious Christian potentate(s) of the Indies by circumnavigating Africa. This Bull also recognized the commercial motive inherent in the Portuguese expansion by granting the King of Portugal and his successors the monopoly of the trade with the inhabitants of the newly-discovered regions, subject to the proviso that the sale of war materials to enemies of the

Faith was forbidden. Finally, it may be mentioned that as the Portuguese pushed their exploratory voyages down the west coast of Africa, they added the acquisition of Negro slaves to Guinea gold, and the search for spices to that for Prester John. The spices, however, only appear as a major motive after the death of Prince Henry in 1460, by which time the west African slave-trade was an established fact.

The Portuguese voyages of discovery and trade down the west coast of Africa commenced systematically in 1433, and a great spurt of progress was made during the eight-year regency (1440–48) of Prince Pedro, elder brother of the better-publicized Prince Henrique, belatedly and somewhat inappropriately named The Navigator. Nevertheless, the latter's share in this enterprise was, admittedly, more important in the long run, since the voyages themselves, and the colonization of the Açores and Madeira, which began a few years earlier, were largely financed from the revenues of the military Order of Christ, of which Dom Henrique was the administrator and governor (but not Grand Master) from 1420 until his death forty years later. Some of the leading Lisbon merchants also had a hand in financing and organizing these voyages. From 1470 to 1475 they were leased on a monopoly-contract basis to a certain Fernão Gomes, under whose administration a large stretch of the Guinea coast was opened up to Portuguese enterprise and trade. It is still uncertain how much was directly due to government initiative and to resources supplied by the Crown or by the Order of Christ, and how much was due to private enterprise, or to both the Crown and the merchant-adventurers acting in conjunction. But it can be said without undue simplification that right from the beginning, the planning, organization, and financing of these voyages owed a great deal to intelligent government initiative and support, as personified in the activities of Dom Henrique. Dom Pedro, and, above all, of Dom João II in the final stages (1481–95). It was this consistent and steady government direction and support which gave the Portuguese the edge over their Spanish neighbours and rivals.[6]

The Spaniards for long contested the papal awards which granted a monopoly of the west African coastal trade to the Portuguese. But save during the years 1475–1480, when they made a determined but unsuccessful attempt to secure the lion's share of the Guinea trade for themselves, the Spanish adventurers did not receive the same consistent and energetic support from their rulers as did the Portuguese from theirs. Moreover, Spain's cereal and financial problems were less acute than those of Portugal for much of the fifteenth century, and therefore the Spaniards had not the same economic incentive to seek new lands to conquer or to exploit. Finally, the existence of the Moorish kingdom of Granada on Andalusian soil, the prior commitments of the Crown of Aragon in the Mediterranean, and the need to strengthen the Crown of Castile against unruly vassals at home, provided powerful distractions which were not present to the same extent in Portugal.

The actual voyages down the west coast of Africa presented no exceptional difficulties to experienced seamen, other than the legendary but none the less real terrors of the unknown. The chief of these were the common (though not unique) belief that the torrid zone was too hot to support life, and that the *Mar Tenebroso*, or "Sea of Darkness"

---

[6] For varying views on Portuguese expansion in the 15th century cf. E. Axelson, *South-East Africa, 1488-1530* (London, 1940); Damião Peres, *Descobrimentos Portugueses* (Porto, 1943); V. Magalhães Godinho, *Documentos sobre a expansão portuguesa* (Lisboa, 1943-56), 3 vols.; A. J. Dinis O.F.M., *Vida e obras de Gomes Eanes de Zurara* (Lisboa, 1949), 2 vols.; Julio Gonçalves, *O Infante Dom Pedro, as Sete Partidas e a génese dos descobrimentos* (Lisboa, 1955); W. J. de Kock, *Portugese ontdekkers om die Kaap* (Kaapstad, 1957); Ch-Martel de Witte, *Les Bulles Pontificales et l'expansion portugaise au XVe siècle* (Louvain, 1958).

south of Cape Nun, was too shallow and dangerous for navigation. Experience soon showed that these beliefs were erroneous, but the real difficulty lay in the return voyage against the northerly winds and currents which usually prevailed along that coast. To avoid these, it was necessary to describe a bold arc into the Atlantic, sweeping near the Açores, which island-group had been discovered, or rather rediscovered, in 1427. From about 1443 the Portuguese sailors facilitated their progress by taking over from Arab or Mediterranean sailors the prototype of the lateen-rigged caravel, which they developed into the handiest type of vessel for their voyages of discovery in the South Atlantic.

As these voyages extended down the coast of Africa and westwards into the Atlantic, the sea experience so gained was fused with the findings of Greek science, as transmitted by Arab and Jewish astronomers and mathematicians, to form the foundations of modern nautical science. By the end of the fifteenth century the best Portuguese navigators could calculate fairly accurately their position at sea by a combination of observed latitude and dead reckoning. They estimated the geographical length of a degree at about 17½ Portuguese leagues (106,560 metres), an error of a little over four per cent, and they possessed excellent practical sailing-directions for the west African coast. Their principal nautical instruments were the mariner's compass (probably derived from the Chinese through Arab and Mediterranean sailors), the astrolabe and the quadrant in their simplest forms, and portulan-type nautical charts[7]

A. Cortesão, 'Nautical science and the Renaissance' *Archives Internationales d'Histoire des Sciences* No. 9, pp. 1075-92, 1949. For more detailed studies, cf. L. de Morais e Sousa, *A sciência náutica dos pilotos Portugueses nos séculos XV e XVI* (Lisboa, 1924), 2 vols., A. Fontoura da Costa, *A marinharia dos descobrimentos* (Lisboa, 1933); Gago Coutinho, *A náutica dos descobrimentos* (Lisboa, 1951-52), 2 vols.; Marcondes de Sousa, 'A astronomia, náutica na época dos descrobrimentos. Ensaio critica', *Revista de História* No. 41, pp. 41-63, 1960.

drawn on a consistent distance-scale but not on a consistent projection. Many of their deep-sea pilots, however, continued to rely chiefly on their knowledge of Nature's signs (*conhecencas*), such as the colour and run of the sea, the types of fish and sea-birds observed in different latitudes, the varieties of seaweed they encountered, and so forth.

Before the Age of Discovery got under way with the finding and colonization of Madeira about 1420, the limits of the known Atlantic world were the Canary Islands and Cape Nun, although (as mentioned previously), it is likely that the most easterly of the Açores and, perhaps, Madeira had been sighted by some forgotten Catalan or Italian pioneers of the thirteenth or fourteenth centuries. By the time Bartolomeu Dias rounded the Cape of Good Hope some sixty-five years later, the Portuguese had colonized the Atlantic islands of the Açores, Madeira, and Cape Verde, as well as São Tomé in the gulf of Guinea. They had explored and charted the west African coast pretty thoroughly as far as 22 southern latitude. It is arguable whether the Portuguese realized before the voyage of Bartolomeu Dias in 1487–88 that the wind system in the south Atlantic was symmetrical with that of the northern hemisphere; but if they were not already aware of this fact, this epoch-making voyage probably gave them the key to open the Cape route to India.

During this period, the Portuguese also made a number of voyages westwards from the Açores; but no reliable details concerning them have survived, and no convincing proof has yet been adduced to show that they had preceeded Columbus in the discovery of America. The most that can safely be said in the present state of our knowledge[8]

[8] S. Morison, *Portuguese voyages to America before 1500* (Harvard University Press, 1940); T. O. Marcondes de Sousa, *Algumas achegas à historia dos descobrimentos marítimos. Críticas e controversias* (São Paulo, 1958).

is that they probably suspected that some continent or islands lay in that direction.

An essential counterpart of the voyage of Bartolomeu Dias was the in some ways even more remarkable overland journey of Pero de Covilhã. This man, an Arabic-speaking squire from Beira, was sent overland to India by King D. João II in the same year that Dias left Lisbon for the Cape. Covilhã was accompanied by another Arabic-speaker, Affonso de Paiva, whose orders were to locate and enter Abyssinia. Paiva perished in this attempt, but Pero de Covilhã between 1487 and 1492 contrived to visit the Malabar Coast of India, the Persian Gulf, the Red Sea, and the eastern coast of Africa as far south, perhaps, as Sofala. He then set out to return to Portugal, but on reaching Cairo, he heard of the death of his companion and received orders from D. João II to complete the latter's mission. After sending back to Lisbon a detailed report on his travels and on the organization of the spice-trade, Pero de Covilhã dutifully turned southwards to try his luck in Abyssinia. More fortunate than Paiva, he penetrated the highland fastnesses of Ethiopia and thus found Prester John, but the Coptic potentate refused to let him leave the country.

As a result of the reports of Bartolomeu Dias and of Pero de Covilhã, D. João II felt pretty sure that the sea-route to India was open, and that Bartolomeu Dias could not have been so very far from Sofala when his mutinous crew had forced him to return home. Just at this point, however, Columbus returned from his famous voyage with the claim that he had reached some islands on the fringe of east Asia after crossing the Atlantic. This unexpected news threatened to upset D. João II's carefully laid plans; but the Portuguese king soon decided that whatever Columbus had discovered, it was not the East Indies for which they were both seeking. The ensuing dispute with the Crown of Castile over prior and other rights of discovery was settled by the Treaty of Tordesillas (1494), by which the Crowns of Portugal and Castile in effect divided the colonial world between them, with the Pope's blessing. D. João II now began preparations for the voyage which was to be commanded by Vasco da Gama, but he died before they were far advanced, and his successor reaped where he had sown.[9]

The fruits of the seeds sown by the Infante Dom Henrique, by King D. João II, and by numerous forgotten pilots and navigators, were reaped by King Manuel I, rightly surnamed "The Fortunate", starting with the voyage of Vasco da Gama in 1497–99. Profiting by the experience of Bartolomeu Dias, if not of other precursors in the South Atlantic, Vasco da Gama, on reaching the latitude of Sierra Leone stood far out into the "Ocean Sea" until the Trade belts were passed, subsequently making a landfall some eighty miles NW of the Cape of Good Hope. This was the first land sighted since he had left the Cape Verdes ninety-six days previously, and this section of the voyage formed the longest passage out of sight of land yet made by a European ship.

After rounding the Cape of Good Hope, and calling at various Arab-Swahili ports along the east coast of Africa, da Gama reached Malindi, where he received the help of Ahmad-Ibn-Madjid, the most famous Arab pilot of his age, and one who knew the Indian Ocean better than any other man living. Thanks to his guidance, the Portuguese were enabled to reach Calicut, the major emporium of the pepper trade on the Malabar Coast, without further difficulties. This voyage inaugurated what a distinguished Indian historian called the Vasco da Gama epoch of Asian history—an age of maritime power, of authority based on

[9] A. Teixeira da Mota, 'A viagem de Bartolomeu Dias e as concepções geopolíticas de D. João II' *Boletim da Sociedade da Geografia de Lisboa*, Sér 76, Nos. 10-12, pp. 297-322, 1958.

the control of the seas by European nations alone. Not unnaturally, Ibn Madjid's memory is still execrated by the majority of his fellow-countrymen and co-religionists; and he himself bitterly bewailed in his old age what he had done.[10]

When the Portuguese finally came ashore at Calicut, some astonished Tunisian traders in the crowd asked them what the devil had brought them so far. "Christians and spices", was the answer allegedly given by da Gama's men, thus showing that whatever motives had originally inspired the Portuguese voyages of discovery after the capture of Ceuta, Christians and spices were what they chiefly hoped to find when they actually reached India. This close association between God and Mammon formed the hallmark of the empire founded by the Portuguese in the East, and, for that matter, in Africa and in Brazil as well.

Thanks to the absence of any strong Asian naval power (save only the Chinese, whose isolationist rulers had deliberately turned their backs on maritime expansion some decades previously), the Portuguese were able to secure the mastery of the Indian Ocean with astonishing speed. The foundations of their Eastern empire were laid by Affonso de Albuquerque, who wrested the land-locked island of Goa from the Muslim Sultan of Bijapur in 1510. He made this place the Portuguese headquarters, a task which was rendered easier by the fact that most of the inhabitants were Hindus and thus had no great love for their former rulers. By the capture of Malacca in 1511, Albuquerque secured the main emporium for the spice-trade, and the strategic key to the South China Sea and to

[10] A. Villiers, *Sons of Sindbad* (London, 1940); K. M. Panikkar, *Asia and Western dominance. A survey of the Vasco da Gama epoch of Asian history, 1498-1945* (London, 1953); T. A. Chumovsky (ed. and trans., M. Malkiel-Jirmounsky), *Três Roteiros desconhecidos de Ahmad Ibn-Mādjid, o piloto Arabe de Vasco da Gama* (Lisboa, 1960).

Indonesia, in fact the sixteenth century equivalent to present-day Singapore. With the seizure of Hormuz in the Persian Gulf in 1515, he obtained control of those waters and of one of the two routes by which the spice-trade was carried on with the Levant. He attempted to block the other route by taking Aden; and though he narrowly failed in this enterprise, the Portuguese could enter the Red Sea at will, even though they never succeeded in closing it to the Muslims. The carrying-trade of the Indian Ocean was in the hands of Muslim traders, mainly Arabs and Gujaratis, at the beginning of the sixteenth century; but the Portuguese quickly ousted some of them and imposed their domination over most of the others. Control of the south-east African coast was secured by establishing fortresses at Sofala and Moçambique. North of Cape Delgado, the Portuguese relied mainly on the loyalty of their oldest Swahili ally, the Sultan of Malindi, until they built Fort Jesus at Mombasa in the last decade of the sixteenth century.[11]

Portuguese naval supremacy in the Indian Ocean was early achieved with Francisco de Almeida's great victory over an Egyptian fleet off Diu (1509), and it was not seriously challenged until the appearance of the Dutch and English in the Indian Ocean nearly a century later. The Muslim rulers of Egypt and Turkey were greatly hampered in their occasional efforts to build fleets for service in the Indian Ocean by the total absence of timber on the shores of the Red Sea and the Persian Gulf. The Arab ships which operated from those regions were built with either Indian or east African timber, which formed part of their return cargoes. So far as the Mamelukes and Ottomans were concerned, the wood for the construction of such ships as they did succeed in building east of Suez and Basra

[11] C. R. Boxer and Carlos de Azevedo, *Fort Jesus and the Portuguese in Mombasa*, 1593-1729 (London, 1960).

had to come overland from the Taurus forests near the Syrian coast. Its transport was an exceedingly difficult and costly operation, and the continual land warfare between Sunni Turkey and Shia Persia was a further distraction. During the sixteenth century, the Turks made only four fleeting efforts in the Indian Ocean, but the ships which. they built at long intervals for service in those waters were eventually hunted down and destroyed by the Portuguese.

The three key strong-points of Goa, Hormuz, and Malacca were soon supplemented by a large number of other fortified settlements and trading posts (*feitorias*, Old English, *factories*) extending from Sofala in south east Africa to Ternate in the Moluccas. In addition, the Portuguese were allowed to form a number of unfortified settlements or factories in some regions where the native rulers, or the local officials, allowed them to enjoy what amounted to extra-territorial rights. Examples of these latter were São Tomé de Meliapor on the Coromandel coast, Hooghly in Bengal, and the City of the Name of God of Macau in China, which was founded at the estuary of the Pearl River, 1555–57. In the Indian Ocean and the Persian Gulf, the Portuguese effectively dominated the monsoon trade-routes, as was implied by King Manuel's grandiloquent title of "Lord of the conquest, navigation, and commerce of Ethiopia, India, Arabia and Persia", which he assumed, only a trifle prematurely, in 1501. Trade with certain ports and in certain commodities (of which spices were the chief) was carried on for the benefit of the Portuguese Crown or of its nominees. Elsewhere, indigenous shipping was allowed to ply as before, provided that the owners took out Portuguese licences (*cartazas*) on payment. Unlicensed ships were liable to be seized or sunk, particularly if they belonged to Muslim traders.

East of Malacca the position was very different.

Portuguese ships could sail unchallenged to the Spice Islands through Indonesian waters, but when they tried strong-arm methods on the China Coast they were decisively defeated by the Chinese coastguard fleets. Beyond Malacca the Portuguese were merely one more thread in the existing pattern of trade and intercourse, nor was it long before they had to compete with the Spaniards who were seeking the same goal from the opposite direction. Once the Spaniards realized that Columbus had not discovered the golden realms of Cathay and Zipangu so enthusiastically described by Marco Polo, and before they found the treasures of Aztec Mexico and Inca Peru, one of their chief objects was to get round or get across the new found American continent which barred their way to the silks, silver, and spices of east Asia. This they finally achieved with what must surely rank as the outstanding voyage of all time, the circumnavigation of the globe planned, organized and begun by the Portuguese Fernão de Magalhães in the service of the Crown of Castile, and completed by the Basque Sebastian del Cano, who sailed the little *Victoria* into San Lúcar de Barrameda on 8 September 1522, after an absence of almost exactly three years. Magalhães and his right-hand man (and brother-in-law), the Portuguese Duarte Barbosa, were killed in two singularly futile skirmishes in the Philippine Islands, but not before they had brought their ships across the Pacific and to within easy reach of the Spice Islands, which they both knew all about from their previous service in Malayan waters. Even if Del Cano had not succeeded in bringing his ship back to Seville after loading a cargo of spices at Tidore, the world had to all intents and purposes been encompassed for the first time in the history of humanity when Portuguese and Spaniards met in the Spice Islands. The work which had begun in the Maghreb in 1415 was brought to a triumphant conclusion in the

Moluccas in 1521. In the previous year, a Portuguese embassy from India at last made contact with the court of Prester John, where Pero de Covilhã was found to be living in honoured old age, and the identity of Abyssinia was definitely established.

The Portuguese empire in Asia and Africa—and to a lesser extent in Brazil, which had been discovered in 1500, and sparsely settled along the coast in the ensuing years— can be described as a commercial and maritime empire cast in a military and ecclesiastical mould. The viceroy at Goa was invariably selected from the military nobility, who also provided the captains of fortresses and governors of settlements, even where these towns were purely commercial. The usual term of office was triennial, and it was an understood thing that occupants of Crown posts would use their positions to fill their pockets, paper safeguards to the contrary notwithstanding. Every male Portuguese who went out to the *Estado da India* (which comprised at its zenith the Portuguese forts and trading posts from Sofala to Nagasaki) did so in the service of the Crown or of the Church. As the overseas church had been placed by fifteenth century Popes under the patronage (*padroado*) of the Portuguese kings in their capacity of Grand Masters of the Order of Christ, it can be said that every male Portuguese who sailed in the annual India Fleets left Lisbon in the service of the Crown. Laymen who married after reaching India were allowed to leave the royal service and settle down as citizens or traders, being then termed *casados* or married men. The remainder were classified as *soldados* (soldiers) and were liable for military service until they died, married, deserted, or were incapacitated by wounds or disease.

The soldiers and government officials were all in receipt of pay and allowances from the Crown, but the Crown's resources were insufficient to provide for either adequate

18

or regular payment to several thousand individuals. The result was that everyone from viceroy to cabin-boy sought to supplement his income by trading; so that virtually every man in Portuguese Asia became either a full-time or a part-time merchant.[12] This example even affected many of the regular and secular clergy, whose stipends were often paid in trade-goods. Few of them achieved more than a mediocre morality, until after the arrival of the Jesuits (1542) who set and maintained much higher standards. The low standard of the clergy as a whole did not prevent their being held in the greatest respect by the Crown, the government officials, and the Indo-Portuguese population in general, partly due to the deep-seated Lusitanian conviction that the "worst religious is better than the best layman".[13]

We have no exact figures for the Portuguese overseas population in the sixteenth and seventeenth centuries, but it would seem that there were never more than between six and seven thousand able-bodied men in service (or

[12] Elaine Sanceau (ed.), *Cartas de Dom João de Castro* (Lisboa, 1954), pp. 28, 41, 42, 55-56, 306-07 (". . . porque todo o homē que quá anda se fez chatím, e andam buscando sua vida por toda a India sem a isso se poder dar remedio"). Similar criticisms of the attitude of the clergy were made as early as 1514 by the first Vicar of Malacca: "E eles craramente me disserão que a principall cousa por que vynhão hà Ymdia nom hera senão por levarem muitos cruzados, dizendo o padre que se não contentaria se ao cabo dos tres annos nom tevese feitos, 5,000 cruzados, e muitas perolas e muitos rubyns" (Letter of Affonso Martins, Cochin, 17 December 1514, in *Studia. Revista Semestral*, Vol. 1, pp. 111-17, 1958.)

[13] Martim Affonso de Miranda, *Tempo de Agora* (Lisboa, 1622-24), 2 vols. Vol. 1, p. 123, and Vol. 2, pp. 77-84, of the reprint of 1785. The same theme repeatedly occurs in Portuguese colonial literature. Cf. Nuno Marques Pereira, *Compendio narrativo do Peregrino da America* (Lisboa, 1769), pp. 234-35. An anonymous account of Moçambique and Zambesia in the mid 17th century stated that the Dominican friars extorted large sums of money from the Portuguese settlers, "que como filhos da egreja lhes tem muito respeito e deixam levar sem remedio; sendo que se não deixam avexar dos ministros d'el rei quando se lhes quer fazer vexame" (*apud* J. de Andrade Corvo, *Estudos sobre as provincias ultramarinas* (Lisboa, 1883-87, 4 vols. Vol. II, p. 108).

liable thereto) in the *Estaao da India*. About half of these were usually deserters, or else had settled in native kingdoms (China, Pegu, Siam, Orissa, Bengal) where they were beyond the control of the viceroy of Goa.[14] To this figure must be added another few thousand men for west Africa, Morocco and Brazil; but the death-rate from tropical diseases in Asia and Africa was excessively high, and that from battle by no means negligible. It is unlikely that there were ever more than 10,000 able-bodied Portuguese men overseas in an empire which extended from South America to the Spice Islands, during the sixteenth century. The population of Portugal at this period probably oscillated at around a million, and a heavy annual emigration from the mother country was needed to fill the gaps caused by the wastage in the tropics. Relatively few female emigrants left Portugal during that century, and of those women who did go, the greater part probably went to Brazil. The voyage from Lisbon to Brazil seldom exceeded two or three months, and was usually made in favourable conditions of wind and weather. On the other hand, the *Carreira da India*, as the round voyage between Lisbon and Goa was called, usually took about six or seven months in either direction, often without touching anywhere on the way, and in weather which ranged from the burning calms of the Gulf of Guinea to the cold and stormy waters off the Cape of Good Hope. Mortality on board the crowded East Indiamen was consequently very heavy, losses of fifty per cent being not unusual. For example, the Fleet of 1571 reached Goa with only about half of the 4,000 men who had embarked at Lisbon.[15]

[14] Cf. The complaints of Affonso de Albuquerque in 1513 (*Cartas*, Vol. I, p. 126), of Dom João de Castro in 1540 (*Cartas*, pp. 25-27, 55-56), and of Martim Affonso de Mello in 1565 (*apud* A. da Silva Rego, *Documentação. India*, Vol. 9, p. 539).
[15] Diogo do Couto, *Decada IX*, ch. 11; Manuel Severim de Faria, *Noticias de Portugal* (Lisboa, 1655), pp. 13-14, 242.

The number of able-bodied Portuguese men in the empire was thus only about the same as that of the present-day Portuguese colony in Johannesburg. This figure is extremely small when we consider that the Portuguese were trying to plant agricultural settlements along the coast of Brazil, in addition to their fighting, trading, and colonizing activities from Morocco to Japan. The wonder is not that their Eastern empire ultimately collapsed, but that it flourished for exactly a century and lasted for as long as it did.

Plate 2 (i)   **The wife of a Portuguese fidalgo**
(from an Indo-Portuguese drawing of *c*. 1540 in the Bibl. Casanatense,
Rome, Cod. 1889, by courtesy of Padre G. Schurhammer S.J.)

Plate 2 (ii)   **A Portuguese fidalgo**
(from an Indo-Portuguese drawing of *c*. 1540 in the Bibl. Casanatense,
Rome, Cod. 1889, by courtesy of Padre G. Schurhammer S.J.)

II

THE CLASH OF COLOUR, CASTE, AND CREED IN THE SIXTEENTH CENTURY

The clash of colour, caste, and creed which inevitably resulted from the irruption of the Portuguese and of militant Roman Catholic Christianity on to the African, Asian, and South American scenes naturally assumed different forms, which I can only briefly discuss here. In Morocco, the crusading spirit lingered on long after it had ceased to have the slightest practical relevance. The main effect of the Portuguese action in conquering Ceuta, Tangier, and a number of other strongholds on the Atlantic coast, was to reinforce the isolation and to intensify the xenophobia of that fanatically Muslim land. The fight against the Portuguese invaders was instigated, organized, and led by the Marabouts, thus giving the struggle the character of a holy war. The last offensive effort of the Portuguese ended in total disaster on the field of Alcaçer-Kebir (4 August 1578), when King D. Sebastião was slain and virtually all of his army who were not killed were taken prisoners. Several of the Portuguese Moroccan strongholds had been abandoned during the reign of D. João III, and by the end of the century only Ceuta, Tangier, and Mazagan remained in Portuguese hands. The garrisons of these three places, who were almost invariably underpaid, underfed, and undermanned, limited themselves to a defensive war of petty skirmishing. They reconnoitred and occasionally raided the surrounding country in day time, seldom venturing beyond sight of the walls, behind which they retired as soon as they were attacked by superior forces.

This intermittent warfare was punctuated by occasional truces, during which a barter-trade was carried on with Moorish and Jewish merchants. These three strongholds were a grievous burden to the Portuguese Crown, which frequently had to find reinforcements and supplies at short notice, when the Moors pressed home their attacks or laid siege in force to one or another of them.[1]

Coming farther down the west coast of Africa to Mauretania and below, the search for Guinea gold was soon reinforced by the demand for slaves. The slave-trade became the principal activity of the Portuguese on the coast after the development of sugar plantations, firstly in Madeira, then in São Tomé, and finally in Brazil. The Spanish Caribbean colonies, and, to a lesser extent, Mexico and Peru, also became profitable slave-markets for Portuguese traders. Although violence was first used to obtain these slaves, the Portuguese soon found that peaceful trade with the Arab, Berber, and Negro agents from the hinterland was more profitable than sudden raids on undefended and unsuspecting coastal villages. The first factory or *feitoria* was founded at Arguim in 1445. This was the prototype of its kind, subsequently adopted—or adapted—by the Dutch, French, and English successors of the Portuguese. Here European textiles, hardware, hides, looking-glasses, etc., were bartered for gold-dust, Negro slaves, gumlac, civet, and a pungent pepper-like spice called malagueta, or "grains of Paradise".

From Cape Verde to the Gold Coast, a rather different system was employed after the Cape Verde Islands had been colonized in the fourteen-sixties. Individual Portuguese traders and exiles frequented the rivers and creeks of Senegambia and Upper Guinea, often settling in the Negro villages, where they and their Mulatto descendants

---

[1] R. Ricard, *Etudes sur l'histoire des Portugais au Maroc* (Coimbra, 1955).

functioned as principals or as intermediaries in the barter-trade for gold and slaves between Black and White. The *Tangomaos*, or *Lançados*, as these men who "went native" were called, included many "fugitives and men banished for committing most heinous crimes and incestuous acts, their lives and conversation being agreeable", as a sixteenth-century Englishman noted.[2] But they were not lacking in courage and initiative, and a few may have penetrated as far inland as the great Sudanese mart of Timbuktu, which was also reached by some envoys of King D. João II. What was, perhaps, more important, and was certainly more lasting, was that they spread the use of the Portuguese language as a commercial lingua franca all along the coast.

On the 150-mile streach of the Gold Coast, the Portuguese relied less on peaceful contacts than on a display of power and force, which, however, they seldom had to use. This region was the most important of all, as it contained some gold-fields in the tropical coastal belt, whereas the gold secured at Cape Verde and Senegambia came from a mysterious district in the western Sudan which was never accurately identified. In 1481, Dom João II, an enthusiastic and far-sighted imperialist if ever there was one, ordered the construction of a strong castle on the European model, at a place subsequently known as São Jorge da Mina, St George of the Mine (Elmina). His objectives in erecting this, the first European stronghold in the tropics, were the domination of the local Negro tribes, and the defence of this gold-producing region against Spanish and other European interlopers. The local chief was none too pleased when the Portuguese began the construction of this castle in January 1482, but the inhabitants of the few neighbouring villages subsequently became converted to Christianity and

---

[2] J. W. Blake, *Europeans in West Africa, 1450-1560* (London, 1942), 2 vols. Vol. I, p. 31, quoting Richard Rainolds' account of 1591.

remained loyal adherents to the Portuguese until the Dutch capture of the castle in 1637.

The famous Portuguese chronicler, João de Barros, who visited Mina as a young man, wrote glowingly of the Portuguese position in Guinea in his *Decada Primeira*, published in 1552: [3]

As far as the increase of the royal patrimony is concerned, I do not know in Portugal of any land-tax, toll, tithe, transfer-tax, or any other crown tax more certain, nor one which yields a more regular annual revenue, with no tenant alleging drought or loss, than what is yielded by the trade of Guinea. And this is such, that if we only knew how to cultivate and harvest it properly, with a little seed it would give us a better yield than do the crown lands of this kingdom and the water-meadows of the vale of Santarem. And moreover it is so peaceful, meek, and obedient an estate, that, without our having one hand holding a lighted lunt on the touch-hole of a gun and the other hand holding a lance, it gives us gold, ivory, wax, hides, sugar, pepper, malagueta; and it would give us more things if we would only penetrate into the hinterland, as we have penetrated to beyond the Japanese people, who are, as it were, the Antipodes or Antichtones, when compared with us. Finally, it yields a numerous and a good people, faithful Catholics, willing workers, and who help us in our needs. And they are so courageous that with them we have conquered the other regions which we hold and which do not produce the like. If I had been trained in the military art, I would rather go to Guinea and enlist soldiers,

[3] João de Barros, *Decada I*, Livro 3, cap. xii. I have to thank Cdte. A. Teixeira de Mota for drawing my attention to this passage which is reproduced in his stimulating essay, 'Notas sobre a história dos Portugueses na África Negra' *Boletim da Sociedade de Geografia de Lisboa*, Sér. 77, Nos. 1-3, pp. 27-55, 1959.

than to the land of the Swiss. And more's the pity, because the Muslims of Africa, and principally the Sherif of Morocco, in our own day and generation are making greater use of them in warfare than we are doing.

And disregarding the way of life or effeminacy of Asia, whose inhabitants are very vicious in this respect, which Salust denounced long ago as being the cause of corrupting the modesty and sobriety of the Roman people— a fault in which the greater part of the Portuguese nation lies at present—but treating of the fruits of nature which this land of Ethiopia gives without any human artifice, we may well term it the land of nature's delights. For it not only yields those necessary and useful for human life, but it likewise yields souls created in the innocence of their first parents, which, with meekness and obedience bend their necks beneath the evangelic yoke for faith and baptism.

After this rhapsody on Guinea and its Negro inhabitants, Barros concludes with a warning note:

But it seems that for our sins, or for some inscrutable judgement of God, in all the entrances of this great Ethiopia that we navigate along, He has placed a striking angel with a flaming sword of deadly fevers, who prevents us from penetrating into the interior to the springs of this garden, whence proceed these rivers of gold that flow to the sea in so many parts of our conquest.

There was indeed the rub. It was the angel of death with his flaming sword of malaria and other tropical diseases, who made so much of west Africa quite literally a white man's grave in the sixteenth century and for long afterwards. Although, as Barros stated, the Portuguese received considerable quantities of gold on the coast, they found

27

it even more difficult to penetrate to the gold-fields of Mali (Wangara) through the tropical rain-forests of the littoral, than the Moors subsequently did across the sandy wastes of the Sahara.

Despite Barros's commendation of the meek, obedient, and faithful Catholic Negroes of Guinea, those converted to Christianity were, in reality, relatively few in number. As indicated above, they were virtually confined to the inhabitants of the villages in the immediate neighbourhood of Mina, Axim, and the other Portuguese forts. Apart from anything else, there were never more than a very few missionaries scattered between Cape Verde and the Congo, and most of those who did venture into this unhealthy region were quickly killed or incapacitated by the lethal climate. South of the river Zaire, it was another story, at any rate for a time; though here, too, the deadly nature of the climate proved ultimately to be a fatal handicap to any lasting missionary work before the discoveries of medical science in the nineteenth century.[4]

The Portuguese discovered the old kingdom of Congo in the same year that they built São Jorge da Mina on the Gold Coast, and they at first achieved even more encouraging results with the even more pliable Bantu. The rulers of this realm soon adopted Christianity and one of them at least, Dom Affonso I, who reigned from 1506 to 1545, proved himself to be a better Christian than most of his teachers, and an ardent advocate of European religion and civilization. At his request, the early Portuguese embassies and missions to the Congo included not only friars and priests, but skilled workers and artisans, such as blacksmiths, masons, bricklayers, and agricultural labourers. Even two German printers emigrated voluntarily to the Congo in 1492, and several white women were sent

---

[4] Cf. António Brásio C.S.Sp., *Monumenta Missionaria Africana. Africa Ocidental 1471-1646* (Lisboa, 1952-60), 9 vols.

out to teach the local ladies the arts of domestic economy as practised in Portugal. A number of Congolese noble youths were sent to Lisbon for their education, and one of them was consecrated a bishop by the Pope, on King Manuel's insistence.

This monarch and his successors of the House of Aviz, did not attempt to secure political control of the kingdom of Congo, nor did they try to conquer it by force of arms. They were content to recognize the kings of Congo as their brothers in arms, and to treat them as allies and not as vassals. Unfortunately, this promising experiment broke down after Dom Affonso I's death, chiefly because of Portugal's rapidly growing commitments in two other continents, and also owing to the spread of the slave-trade. "Black ivory" quickly became, and for centuries remained, the principal European concern with the west African coast, and the Portuguese were the pioneers in this as in other respects. Nevertheless, the Lusitanian cultural imprint given in the sixteenth century lasted for a long time in the Congo. A nominal form of Christianity survived here until well into the eighteenth century, and many of the leading men could speak, read, and write Portuguese fluently until at least as late as the mid-seventeenth century.[5]

The attitude of the Portuguese towards the natives of Angola and Benguela forms a curious contrast with the efforts so persistently made to convert and civilize the Congolese by peaceful means. The inhabitants of the country south of the river Bengo were admittedly far less advanced than those of the old kingdom of Congo when the Portuguese first made enduring contacts with them, but this does not entirely explain the summary way in which they were treated for the most part. Disillusionment at the meagre results

[5] Cf. J. Cuvelier and L. Jadin, *L' Ancien Congo d'après les archives romaines 1518-1640* (Bruxelles, 1954); J. Cuvelier, *L'ancien royaume du Congo* (Bruges, 1946).

obtained after such a promising start in the Congo evidently had a good deal to do with it. As early as 1568 a pioneer Jesuit missionary in Angola advocated what one of his colleagues in Brazil termed "preaching with the sword and rod of iron".[6] Padre Francisco de Gouveia, who was detained for some years at the kraal of the Ngola, or native chief from whom Angola derives its name, explained that the Bantu were barbarous savages who could not be converted by the methods of peaceful persuasion which were employed with such cultured Asian nations as the Japanese and Chinese. Christianity in Angola, he wrote, must be imposed by force, though once the Bantu were converted, they would make excellent Christians.

This advocacy of the Church Militant fitted in well enough with the proposals of Paulo Dias de Novais, who was then pressing his scheme for the conquest and colonization of Angola upon a somewhat hesitant court. The charter which was finally given him by the Crown in 1571 has been adequately analysed by Professor Silva Rego, and there is no deed to discuss it here.[7] Suffice it to say that this charter envisaged the colonization of at least a part of Angola by peasant families from Portugal, who were to be provided with "all the seeds and plants which they can take from this kingdom and from the island of São Tomé". But when Paulo Dias's expedition arrived off Luanda in February 1575, the slave-trade there was already in full swing; the lethal climate proved an insuperable obstacle to white colonization; and the high ideals of the charter

---

[6] ". . . para este genero de gente não há melhor pregação do que espada e vara de ferro" (letter of Joseph de Anchieta S.J., d. 23 April 1563); cf. the letter of Padre Mauricio Serpe S.J. to the Jesuit General at Rome, dated 1560, *apud* A. Brásio, *Monumenta missionaria Africana. Africa Ocidental* (Lisboa, 1952-60), Vol. 2, pp. 566-69, 1953.

[7] A. da Silva Rego, *Portuguese Colonization in the Sixteenth century. A study of the Royal Ordinances (Regimentos)* (Johannesburg, 1958), pp. 97-116.

were soon abandoned for the unrestrained procurement of *peças*, "pieces", as Negro slaves were termed.

This demand for slaves intensified and perpetuated the inter-tribal wars which raged in the interior, and in which the cannibal Jagas played such a prominent part. The Portuguese had aided successive kings of the Congo against these barbarous invaders, who, at one time, had sacked the capital itself and who had only been driven off by timely assistance from São Tomé. In Angola, however, the Jagas were mostly on good terms with the white men; and they formed the backbone of the *guerra preta* or native auxiliaries (*empacasseiros*), with whose aid the Portuguese dominated the other tribes. These latter frequently revolted, only to be subdued again by punitive expeditions whose savage reprisals provoked further rebellions; and this dreary round of fighting, slave-raiding and slave-trading continued for over two centuries.

This procedure was criticized in Portugal by the scholarly Canon of Evora Cathedral, Manuel Severim de Faria, who observed sorrowfully that:

one cannot yet see any good effect resulting from so much butchery; for this is not the way in which commerce can flourish and the preaching of the gospel progress, which is what is needed in that State.[8]

These views were not shared by most of those on the spot, as can be seen from a perusal of the fascinating work of António de Oliveira de Cadornega, *Historia des Guerras*

[8] ". . . Tal foi a matança que se fez nos naturaes da terra, posto que se não veja ainda o bom effeito que hade resultar de tanta carneçaria, porque não he este a via para florescer o comercio nem pregarse o evangelho, que he o que naquelle Estado se requere." The same author observed in his *Noticias de Portugal* (Evora, 1655, but written about thirty years earlier): "Em Angola desde o anno de 1575, em que começou a conquista, ategora tudo forão guerras, e da conversão dos naturais se tratou pouco." (cf. op. cit., pp. 226-27, 235-36). Cf. also Ralph Delgado, *Historia de Angola* (Benguela and Lobito, 1948-55), 4 vols. Vol. III, p. 216.

Angolanas, written by him at Luanda in 1680, after over forty years' experience of the colony. He was never tired of stressing that "all these heathen peoples are not ruled nor do they obey through love, but only through sheer force". Quoting with approval the advice of António de Abreu de Miranda, captain-major of the fortress of Ambaca, to the governor of Angola in 1640, Cadornega wrote that only drastic measures with Negroes were of any avail:

for these heathen, more than those of any other nation, act on the principle of "long live the winner", and as Negroes they fear nothing save only corporal punishment and the whip, as was the case with the Romans and the Libertines, when the former could not subdue the latter by force of arms but only by the lash with which they punished and whipped them. It is only in this way that the former governors and conquerors kept them in subjection, and only in this way can we keep what we have won by force of arms in these kingdoms.[9]

In short, Cadornega's attitude to the Negro was just the opposite to that voiced by João de Barros and by Manuel Severim de Faria; but there is no doubt that the colonists' viewpoint prevailed in practice over the humanitarian sentiments which were sometimes voiced in the mother-country.

On the other side of Africa the picture changes again. The Portuguese pioneers found the east coast from Sofala to Somalia occupied by a chain of Arab-Swahili coastal settlements, strongly Africanized by centuries of contact and concubinage with the Bantu, but proudly conscious of their Islamic civilization. They traded with the Bantu tribes of the hinterland for gold, ivory, and to a lesser degree, slaves, giving them in exchange chiefly beads

[9] António de Oliveira de Cadornega, *História Geral des Guerras Angolanas*, *1680* (Lisboa, 1940-42), 3 vols. Vol. I, pp. 260-61. Cf. also Vol. I, pp. 91-92; Vol. III, p. 40.

and cotton textiles, both of Indian origin. The Portuguese almost at once identified Sofala with the Biblical Ophir, and they endeavoured to monopolize the gold-trade of that place by building a fort there in 1505. By fair means and by foul they tried to displace the Swahili traders and to deal direct with the Negroes who brought the gold from the interior, but their efforts, whether forcible or otherwise, met with only partial success. The Swahili had been established there too long and were too numerous to be driven away from all the coastal creeks and islands, let alone the rivers and the bush of the mainland, by such scanty forces as the Portuguese could muster. Moreover, the arrival of the Portuguese more or less coincided with the beginnings of the dissolution of the Makalanga tribal confederacy the "Empire of Monomotapa", as the Portuguese grandiloquently termed it in the expectation of finding an African El Dorado. This led to frequent inter-tribal wars in the interior which greatly impeded, when they did not altogether stop, the flow of gold to the coast; and they rendered it very difficult for the Portuguese traders to penetrate into the interior. Finally, as on the west coast, the deadly fevers of the littoral (and of the Zambezi river valley) took an enormous toll of European lives, which often reached catastrophic proportions.

Nevertheless, despite all these obstacles, and others which I have no space to mention, the Portuguese did secure a considerable quantity of gold, though not nearly as much as they got from São Jorge da Mina. Many visitors to Portugal have seen the golden monstrance at Belem, which was made by the goldsmith-poet, Gil Vicente, with the first consignment of east African gold to reach Lisbon (1506). But subsequently very little of this gold got as far as the Tagus, at any rate of that which belonged to the Crown, for this was earmarked for the purchase of pepper for the homeward-bound Indiamen on the Malabar Coast of India. The official correspondence of the period abounds with complaints that whereas Sofala "gave nothing in excess to the Crown save expenses" (as Albuquerque wrote in 1510), many of the governors and other officials made fortunes through contraband trading in gold. Apart from those who brought back their illicit gains to India or, more rarely, to Lisbon, there were many adventurers who spent their lives in the bush, trading for gold and ivory with the Bantu, in much the same way as did the *lançados* and *tangomaos* in Guinea and Senegambia. Most of these men, of course, are not known to us by name; but the researches of Eric Axelson, Hugh Tracey, and Alexandre Lobato have recently uncovered something about one of the most remarkable of them—the convict ship's carpenter, António Fernandes, who penetrated deep into what is now Southern Rhodesia, and was regarded by the warring Bantu as being semi-divine.[10]

In contrast to what was happening on the west coast of Africa, the Portuguese were not primarily interested in the slave-trade on the east coast during the sixteenth century. They always did trade in slaves, of course, but these were required only as domestic servants or bodyguards; so the numbers involved were nothing like as large as those exported from the west coast to satisfy the voracious demands of the sugar plantations and the silver mines of South and Central America. Gold and ivory were the staples of the east African trade in the sixteenth century, and the principal Portuguese efforts were made along the Zambezi

[10] E. Axelson, *South-East Africa, 1488-1530* (London, 1940); Hugh Tracey, *António Fernandes, descobridor do Monomotapa, 1514-1515, tradução Portuguesa e notas por* Caetano Montez (Lourenço Marques, 1940); Alexandre Lobato, *A expansão Portuguesa em Moçambique 1498-1530* (Lisboa, 1954-60), 3 vols. Cf. also W. A. Godlonton, 'The journeys of António Fernandes—the first known European to find the Monomotapa and to enter Southern Rhodesia' *Proceedings and Transactions of the Rhodesia Scientific Association*, Vol. 40, pp. 71-103, April 1945.

river valley from about 1530 onwards, after Sofala had fallen into irredeemable decay.

Of the Swahili settlements at which Vasco da Gama touched in 1498–99, Malindi remained the faithful ally (or satellite, as we would say nowadays) of the Portuguese Crown for more than a century; but Mombasa, Kilwa, and some of the other ports offered open or covert resistance at one time or another. How the Portuguese dealt with this opposition was recorded by a Spanish envoy to the Shah of Persia, who passed that way over a hundred years later:

> Some years after the Portuguese began their annual voyages to India, with the inborn hatred that their soldiers and seamen had for all Muslims, they not only sacked, burnt, and destroyed those settlements, but barbarously put all the inhabitants to the sword, without distinction of age or sex. Even nowadays, these islanders, who are half-breed Kaffirs and Arabs, preserve the memory of the great terror caused by the wounds which the Portuguese gave with their swords.[11]

But the Spaniard also noted that some Portuguese, attracted by the ivory and the slave trades, were settled on the Swahili coast and offshore islands, where they had inter-married, or at any rate interbred with both Bantu and Swahili women. It would not be a gross over-simplification to say that here, as in many places, Portuguese activities consisted of alternately fighting, trading, and fornicating with the local inhabitants. Missionaries of various Orders were active along the coast and in the Zambezi river valley, but although they achieved some success among the heathen Bantu, they had none worth mentioning among the Swahili. As in all Muslim regions from Morocco to

---

[11] *Comentarios de D. Garcia de Silva y Figueroa* (Madrid, 1905), 2 vols., Vol. 2, pp. 530-31. Cf. also Fr. João dos Santos O.P., *Ethiopia Oriental* (Evora, 1909), Part 1, Book 3, chapter 5, for an almost identical observation by a man on the spot.

Mindanao, the only lasting result of Christian missionary work was to strengthen the influence of Islam.

Coming farther up the coast, the Portuguese wisely left the warlike and fanatical Somali severely alone; and when they finally made contact with the Negus of Abyssinia in 1520, they were naturally disappointed to find that Prester John was only the semi-barbarous potentate of a poor highland kingdom. Still, their military intervention at a critical period in 1541–43 did save Abyssinia from being overrun by the Turks, and, in all probability, from extinction as a Christian state. The Jesuit mission which they subsequently established achieved some success for a time, and gave to Europe several valuable works on the country by reliable and experienced observers.[12] But the Jesuits were expelled in 1633, and the only lasting result of their self-sacrificing labour in this mission - field was to confirm the Abyssinians in their Coptic creed and in their dislike of Roman Catholic Christianity.

The Portuguese never occupied the entrance to the Red Sea, but their control of the Persian Gulf was secured by their occupation of Hormuz, and strengthened by the building of a fort at Muscat in 1587. The Shah of Hormuz had been a Portuguese puppet since Albuquerque's day, but the strength of Islam in this region was sufficient to prevent the Portuguese from destroying all the mosques on Hormuz Island, as they did elsewhere in their possessions wherever they had the chance.

Portuguese policy in India, as inaugurated by Affonso de Albuquerque, was at first to favour or at least tolerate the Hindus, while actively persecuting the adherents of Islam. This policy was soon subjected to serious modifica-

[12] Francisco de Alvares, *Verdadeira informaçam das terras do Preste Joam* (Lisboa, 1540); Balthasar Telles, *Historia geral de Ethiopia a alta ou Preste Joam* (Coimbra, 1660); Pero Pais, *Historia de Etiopia*, ed.. L. Teixeira, (Porto, 1945). Alvares was not a Jesuit.

tions, as the Portuguese found it was impossible to do without the services or the assistance of Muslims in many instances, as, for example, in the employment of Gujarati and Arab sailors in their shipping, and of Swahili intermediaries in some branches of the east African trade. With the arrival of the Jesuits (1542) and the establishment of the Inquisition (1560), the heat was turned on the Hindus and Buddhists as well, their temples and sacred buildings being systematically destroyed in most places where the Portuguese exercised effective power. One notable exception was Diu, where the Hindus were allowed to retain and repair their existing temples, though not to build new ones. This privilege was often assailed by the more bigoted of the clergy, but they did not succeed in abolishing it. One of the reasons for its retention in spite of these attacks, was the assistance given to the Jesuit Patriarch of Ethiopia, D. Affonso Mendes, by Hindu merchants from Diu at a time when the Jesuits were being expelled from Abyssinia and imprisoned by the Turks. In return for their help, D. Affonso Mendes secured the preservation of the precarious privileges enjoyed by the Hindus at Diu.[13] A rather different example was afforded by the action of the Chinese authorities at Canton, who refused to allow the demolition of Chinese temples, or the suppression of Buddhist religious processions at Macau, thus compelling the Portuguese to tolerate these heathen rites there.

Contrary to what is often asserted, the Portuguese did not seek to impose Roman Catholic Christianity at the point of the sword; but they did seek to foster their religion through coercive and discriminatory legislation. The enforcement of these laws in favour of Roman Catholic

[3] Cf. *Archivo Portuguez Oriental*, Fasc. VI (Nova Goa, 1875), pp. 1012, 1254-55; *Arquivo Portugues Oriental* (Nova Edição), (Bastorá, 1938), Tomo IV, Vol. II, Parte II, pp. 640-59.

Christianity inevitably varied widely in time and place. The enactment which gave the most offence was that all orphan children should be taken from their relations and brought up in Christian institutions or households. Since any child whose father had died was classified as an orphan, even if the mother was still alive, this law naturally caused many family tragedies and much hardship. The first Ecclesiastical Council which was celebrated at Goa in 1567 also enacted that all Christians, whether white or coloured, should have no social contacts with Muslims, Hindus, Buddhists, or with Gentiles in general. Intermarriage with adherents of these religions was, of course, forbidden; and all contacts with non-Christians were to be limited to essential business dealings only. It need hardly be said that this injunction to what is nowadays termed *apartheid* was largely ignored in practice, though successive ecclesiastical councils held at Goa in the sixteenth and seventeenth centuries urged the colonial government to implement the decisions of 1567.

These ecclesiastical councils likewise stressed the desirability of government posts and pickings being given to native Christians rather than to Hindus and Muslims. This was indeed the Crown's policy, as exemplified by numerous edicts; but the frequency with which these edicts were issued indicates how ill they were often observed. The tax-farmers and collectors for long remained principally Hindus in Portuguese India, in much the same way as Jews had filled the parallel posts in Europe, and for the same basic reason—their superior financial acumen and abilities. On the other hand, the edicts against toleration of Hindu and Buddhist priests, and of Muslim Imams and Mullahs, and against the use of the sacred books of these religions, were usually strictly enforced. Similarly, temples, shrines, mosques and sacred places were often destroyed by the Portuguese, so that the practice of any religion other than Roman Catholic Christianity became very difficult, and at times impossible, on Portuguese colonial soil. This undoubtedly aided the process of converting the local inhabitants to Christianity, and goes far to account for those 'pockets' of Roman Catholic communities which have survived till to-day in some regions of the west coast of India, Ceylon, and Malacca.[14]

The establishment of the Portuguese power in three continents was greatly facilitated by the inter-tribal, inter-racial, or international rivalries which prevailed at the time of their appearance on the scene, and which enabled them to get and to maintain, or to expand, a foothold. In east Africa, for example, they supported the sultans of Malindi against the more powerful rulers of Mombasa in the sixteenth century, and in the next century they helped the princes of Faza against their overweening neighbours of Pate. On the Malabar Coast, they supported the Rajah of Cochin against the stronger Samorin of Calicut, and in 1683 Goa was rescued by an army of the Great Moghul from what appeared to be its certain capture by the Marathas. In Ceylon, the traditional rivalry between Sinhalese and Tamils, which has flared up again recently, helped the Portuguese to make numerous converts among the latter, particularly in the kingdom of Jaffnapatam. One of the favourite allegations of modern Sinhalese nationalists is that the Tamils co-operated more willingly with the successive Portuguese, Dutch, and English over-lords of Ceylon, and were rewarded for their collaboration by government posts and other privileges. These allegations are doubtless exaggerated, but they do reflect the fact that

[14] *Primeiro concilio de Goa* (Goa, 1568); *Archivo Portuguez Oriental* (Nova Goa, 1862), Part 4; A. da Silva Rego, *Documentação para a história das missões do padroado português do Oriente. India* (Lisboa, 1952-58), 12 vols.; *O Oriente Português* Nos. 7-9, pp. 188-214, especially dispatch on p. 201, 1934-35.

European civilization and religions found a less reluctant acceptance with the Tamils than they did with the Sinhalese.

In Malaya, Indochina, and Indonesia, Portuguese power and consequently Portuguese influence, was inevitably weaker than it was on the coasts of Africa and of the Indian subcontinent. Neither in Buddhist Indochina nor in Muslim Malaya and Indonesia did Roman Catholic Christianity make any striking progress, if we except the formation of sizeable Christian communities in Tongking and Annam. These in their early stages were largely the work of Portuguese Jesuits of the Japan mission, which had been closed to them by the expulsion of the Portuguese from the island-empire in 1639. In Muslim Malaya and Indonesia, the principal effect of the impact of militant Roman Catholic Christianity, as introduced by the Portuguese, was to sharpen the resistance and to spread the influence of Islam. Only in Amboina and in some of the Lesser Sunda Islands (Solor, Timor, Flores, Ende) did the Portuguese missionaries achieve any lasting successes, and there only in certain limited regions which had not been seriously affected by Islam. Their establishment in the Moluccas, and their subsequent tenure there, which was always of a precarious nature, were likewise due in great part to the traditional rivalry between the Sultans of Ternate and Tidore, and to the age-old inter-clan rivalries which prevailed in Amboina and Halmahera.[15]

On the other hand, Portuguese cultural influence in the Spice Islands was in many ways more lasting than that of their Dutch successors, who had a far firmer grip on the Moluccas and who ruled there for nearly three and a half centuries, as against less than one hundred years of

[15] Artur de Sá, *Documentação para a historia das missões do padroado português do Oriente. Insulíndia, 1506-1595* (Lisboa, 1954-58), 5 vols. J. Keuning, 'Ambonnezen, Portugezen en Nederlanders. Ambon's geschiedenis tot het einde van de zeventiende eeuw' *Indonesië* Vol. 9, No. 2, pp. 135-68, 1956.

Portuguese domination. Yet all European travellers in those regions, from the time of the naturalist William Wallace a century ago, comment on the fact that the Portuguese left a deeper cultural imprint on the inhabitants than did the Dutch.

The Portuguese never exercised any political power in the Far East, but both their trade and their religion at one time flourished exceedingly. Their commercial prosperity in the China Sea during the (near) century 1543–1640, was due principally to the Chinese emperors of the Ming dynasty having previously prohibited all trade and intercourse between their subjects and the Japanese, owing to the frequent piratical attacks made by the latter on the China Coast. This ban was not always strictly enforced, but it was sufficiently effective for most of this period to enable the Portuguese of Macau to secure a more or less official monopoly of the carrying-trade between the two empires, as the Dutch and English found to their annoyance when they tried to 'horn in' on this profitable trade in the first quarter of the seventeenth century. This triangular trade between Canton, Macau, and Nagasaki—supplemented for a time by a 'feeder' line between Macau and Manila—was based principally on the exchange of Chinese silks and gold for Japanese silver and copper.

In addition to these worldly treasures, the Portuguese imported their religion and their fire-arms into both the great Far Eastern empires, though neither of these imports achieved the universal popularity of a third one, tobacco. The Japan mission established originally by St Francis Xavier achieved spectacular success for a time at the turn of the sixteenth century, encouraging the more sanguine Jesuits to hope that the defection of the British Isles from the true faith would be counterbalanced by the total conversion of the Japanese. These hopes were dashed by the systematic persecution inaugurated by the Tokugawa

41

Shoguns in 1613, which virtually drowned the mission in blood before the mid-seventeenth century, though a clandestine form of the faith survived in some isolated rural communities in Kyushu until the reopening of Japan two hundred years later. The China mission got off to a slower start, but made steadier if less spectacular progress in the long run, although the great days of the Jesuits at the Court of Peking were more the work of Italian, German, Flemish, and French missionaries than of their Portuguese colleagues.

The oft-made claim that the Portuguese had no colour-bar cannot be substantiated. The most that can truthfully be said is that in this respect they were usually more liberal in practice than were their Dutch, English, and French successors. The Portuguese religious Orders, like the Spanish, would not admit coloured or half-caste recruits to their ranks for many years, and when they began to do so, they made invidious distinctions. The Jesuits, who originally had no colour-bar in theory, quickly adopted one in Asia and Africa under Portuguese pressure; and where efforts to relax this colour-bar were made, they were usually the work of Italian and not of Portuguese members of the Order. It was the Italian Father-Visitor, Alexandre Valignano, who insisted on the admission of Japanese to the Society in 1582, a concession which he subsequently extended to Chinese and Koreans. But Indians were only admitted much later, and Negroes and Amerindians do not seem to have been admitted at all during the colonial period. At the end of the seventeenth century, a Portuguese Jesuit who had been born in Brazil, but who had worked for many years in the Indian mission-field, complacently referred to "the Portuguese character which naturally despises all these Asiatic races".[16]

[16] Francisco de Sousa, S.J., *Oriente Conquistado* (Lisboa, 1710), 2 vols. C. M. de Melo, S.J., *The recruitment and formation of the native clergy in India, 16th-19th century* (Lisboa, 1955).

As regards the Franciscans, the statutes of their Order prohibited them from admitting novices who were descended from converted Muslims or heathen forbears as far back as the fourth generation. There is no doubt that half-castes were sometimes able to evade this ruling, but only by claiming to be of pure white descent. Even men born of European parents in the East were regarded with disdain by their colleagues born in Portugal, who did not scruple to term them "niggers" and to aver that they were good for nothing. In the 1630's a determined attempt was made by the European-born Franciscan friars to prohibit any friar born of white parents in the East from holding high office in the Order. This attempt was only defeated by the dispatch of an Indian-born (but not Indian) friar to Rome, who took with him an Indian syndic, in order to show the Pope the difference in colour and complexion between a white man born in India and an Indian. This emissary eventually carried his point, and obtained a ruling that friars born of pure white parents in India were not to be discriminated against in any way. But he only obtained this result after intensive lobbying at the Court of Madrid (Portugal being then incorporated with the Spanish Crown) and at Rome, in the teeth of bitter opposition from his Portuguese-born colleagues who were warmly supported by the Count of Linhares, Viceroy of Portuguese India from 1629 to 1635.[17]

The policy of the Portuguese Crown on the colour-bar was not always clear and consistent, but on the whole the Portuguese kings took the line that religion and not colour should be the criterion for full Portuguese citizenship, and that all Asian converts to Christianity should be treated as the equals of their Portuguese co-religionists. This indulgence does not seem to have been extended either to

[17] Fr. Miguel da Purificação O.F.M., *Relação Defensiva dos filhos da India Oriental, e da provincia do apostolo S. Thomé dos frades menores da regular observancia da mesma India* (Barcelona, 1640).

43

Amerindians or to Negroes, although the former were legally prohibited from being enslaved, save under exceptional circumstances and strict safeguards. Slavery, indeed, was one of the main pillars of the Lusitanian empire. The sugar plantations of Brazil, the household labour of the Portuguese settlers in three continents, and even to some extent the defence of their settlements, depended mainly on the strong right arms of their (principally African) slaves.

III

THE STRUGGLE FOR SPICES, SUGAR, SLAVES, AND SOULS IN THE SEVENTEENTH CENTURY

The defeat and death of the childless king Dom Sebastião on the field of Alcaçer Kebir in Morocco (4 August 1578), to which I alluded in the last lecture, led to the seizure of the Portuguese Crown in 1580 by King Felipe II of Spain. His claims, legal and otherwise, to the throne left vacant by the death of the Cardinal-King Henrique in that year, were enforced with the aid of the Duke of Alva's veterans and of Mexican 'silver bullets' in a judicious combination which enabled him to boast of his new domain: "I inherited it, I bought it, and I conquered it" (*Yo lo heredé, Yo lo compré, Yo lo conquisté*). The Crowns of Spain and Portugal remained united for the next sixty years, a period which Portuguese patriots subsequently compared to the Babylonian captivity of the Jews. The Iberian colonial empire which lasted from 1580 to 1640, and which stretched from Macau in China to Potosí in Peru, was the first world empire on which the sun never set.

Felipe's seizure of the Portuguese Crown met with little more than token resistance in 1580. A large part of the nobility was in favour of the union; and the mass of the people, who were sullenly opposed to it, were still disorganized, dispirited, and leaderless after the disaster of Alcaçer-Kebir. Nevertheless, Portuguese national sentiment was strong enough, and Felipe himself was prudent enough, to ensure that at the *Cortes* (Parliament) of Tomar—which gave legal sanction to his seizure of the Crown—it was agreed that the two colonial empires should remain

Plate 3
The Festival of São Gonçalo d'Amarante at Bahia, 1718
(from Le Gentil de la Barbinais, *Nouveau Voyage antour du Monde*
Paris, 1728)

separately administered entities. The union of the two Crowns was a personal one, like that of the United Kingdom of Scotland and England in the persons of the Stuart kings from the accession of James VI (and I) to the Act of Union. King Felipe II (and I) swore to preserve Portuguese laws and language; to consult Portuguese advisers on all matters pertaining to Portugal and its overseas possessions; and to appoint only Portuguese officials in those possessions. Last not least, Spaniards were expressly prohibited from trading or settling in the Portuguese empire, and Portuguese from trading or settling in the Spanish.

Felipe II (I of Portugal), and his successor, Felipe III (II of Portugal), kept the terms of the agreement well enough; but in the reign of Felipe IV, Portuguese privileges began to be whittled away, undermined, or simply over-ridden, as a result of the centralizing policy initiated by his chief minister, the Count-Duke of Olivares. It was Olivares's ambition to construct a strong, centralized Castilian monarchy, as his rival, Richelieu, was doing with the French Crown. This policy brought Olivares into conflict with powerful Portuguese interests, such as the Church and the nobility, which would otherwise not, perhaps, have become actively discontented with rule by Madrid. Nor was the dissatisfaction all on one side. If the Portuguese complained that the Castilian connection had brought on them the hostility of Spain's enemies, particularly the aggression of the Dutch and the English, and that Portuguese troops were used to fight Spanish battles in Flanders and Italy, the Spaniards complained that the Portuguese made insufficient efforts to help themselves. The Spaniards also alleged that while Portuguese Asia was firmly closed to Spanish traders, the Portuguese—and particularly Portuguese Jews—penetrated into the richest regions of Mexico and Peru. The Councillors of the Inquisition at Madrid reflected this belief when they averred

47

(albeit with palpable exaggeration) in 1623 that there were apparently more Portuguese Jews than Spanish colonists in Peru.[1]

Portuguese complaints that the union with Spain had drawn on them the hostility of the Protestant powers, while natural enough, were hardly fair. There is no doubt but that the Dutch and English would eventually have come into conflict with Portugal over the latter's claim that she was the sole mistress of the seas to the east of the Cape of Good Hope, and of most of the South Atlantic as well. Still, the fact remains that it was Felipe II's efforts to suppress the revolt in the Netherlands, and his consequent embargo on Dutch trade with the Iberian empire, which was the immediate cause of Dutch hostilities with Portugal. Moreover, once the Dutch had decided to carry the war overseas, and to attack their enemies in the colonial possessions which gave them the economic resources to wage war on many fronts in Europe, then Portugal, as the weaker partner in the Iberian union, inevitably suffered more than Castile under the blows of superior Dutch sea power. As the struggle went on, the Dutch tended more and more to concentrate on attacking Portuguese possessions in Asia, Africa, and South America. These were nearly all situated on the exposed sea coasts, and hence they were far more vulnerable than the land-based Spanish vice-royalties of Mexico and Peru, which could never be reduced —or even seriously affected—by seaborne attacks alone.

[1] "Ya parece que en las [partes] del Perú son más en número que los pobladores españoles" (*Consulta* of the Consejo de la Inquisición at Madrid, 31 March 1623, on a dispatch from the Lima Inquisitors, *apud* R. Konetzke, *Colección de documentos para la historia de la formación social de Hispanoamérica, 1493-1810* (Madrid, 1958), Vol. 2, Book 1, p. 275. On the general question of Portuguese Jews in Spanish America at this period cf. Lorenço de Mendoça, *Supplicacion a su magested catolica del Rey nuestro señor ante sus Reales Consejos de Portugal y de las Indias, en defensa de los Portugueses* (Madrid, 1630).

The Dutch expansion on the Seven Seas during the first half of the seventeenth century was in its way as remarkable as the overseas expansion of Spain and Portugal one hundred years earlier; but I am only concerned now with its devastating effect on the Portuguese empire. The struggle began at the dawn of the seventeenth century, and ended with the capture of the Portuguese settlements on the Malabar Coast in 1663, although the terms of peace were not finally settled until six years later. At the risk of over-simplification, it can be said that this lengthy colonial war took the form of a fight for the spice-trade of Asia, for the slave-trade of west Africa, and for the sugar-trade of Brazil. Similarly, it can be said that the final result was, in effect, a victory for the Dutch in Asia, a draw in west Africa, and a victory for the Portuguese in Brazil. In briefest outline, this struggle in three continents and on five seas can be summarized as follows.

The Dutch early achieved success in the Far East by their capture of the Spice Islands in 1605, against strong Portuguese resistance at Tidore and against no resistance whatever in Amboina. The Spaniards from the Philippines staged a counter-offensive in the following year, which enabled them to seize and retain Tidore and a part of Ternate, until the threat of a Chinese attack on Manila forced them to recall their Moluccan garrisons in 1662. Meanwhile, the Dutch mercilessly harried the Portuguese inter-port trade of Asia—their blockade of the Straits of Malacca in the 1630's being particularly effective—and they reduced many of the long chain of Portuguese coastal settlements by picking them off one by one. Malacca fell in 1641 and the last Portuguese stronghold in Ceylon (Jaffna) seventeen years later. The Asian conquests of the Dutch were rounded off by their capture of Cochin and the other Portuguese settlements on the Malabar Coast in 1663.

In this way, the Dutch had successfully gained control

of the cloves, mace, and nutmegs of the Moluccas, of the cinnamon of Ceylon, and of the pepper of Malabar. They had also displaced the Portuguese in securing the lion's share of the carrying-trade in Asian waters. The Dutch also secured the monopoly of European trade with Japan, after the Portuguese of Macau had been expelled from the island - empire for political and religious motives by the military dictatorship of the Tokugawa in 1639. The Dutch failed only in their efforts to expel the Portuguese from the City of the Name of God of Macau in China, and from the outermost islands of the Lesser Sunda Group (Flores-Solor-Timor) on the edge of the then known world.[2]

In east Africa, the Dutch failed to take the Portuguese way-station of Moçambique Island, and this was one of the reasons which later induced them to found their own settlement at the Cape of Good Hope. In west Africa, the Dutch early established themselves on the Guinea coast; and although they failed disastrously when attempting to capture São Jorge da Mina in 1625, an expedition organized by Count Johan Maurits of Nassau-Siegen, Governor-general of Netherlands Brazil, 1638-1644, accomplished this feat thirteen years later. The Dutch forcibly occupied the coast of Angola and Benguela in 1641, although they knew that Portugal had rebelled against the Spanish connection in the previous December, and that the overseas *conquistas* would in all probability follow the example of the mother-country. The Calvinist invaders established surprisingly cordial relations with the Roman Catholic King of the Congo, and with the cannibal Queen

[2] For detailed accounts cf. N. MacLeod, *De Oost-Indische Compagnie als Zeemogendheid in Azië, 1602-1652* (Rijswijk, 1927), 2 vols. and atlas. A. Botelho de Sousa, *Subsídios para a história militar marítima da India, 1585-1650* (Lisboa, 1930-56), 4 vols.; H. Leitão, *Os Portugueses em Timor e Solor de 1515 a 1702* (Lisboa, 1948); C. R. Boxer, 'Portuguese and Dutch colonial rivalry, 1641-1661', *Studia. Revista Semestral*, Vol. 2, pp. 7-42, 1958.

'Nzinga of the Jagas. In August 1648, these strangely assorted allies were on the point of annihilating the surviving Portuguese defenders of Angola in their three remaining strongholds in the Cuanza valley (Muxima, Massangano, and Cambambe), when a Luso-Brazilian expedition from Rio de Janeiro recaptured Luanda and reversed the situation at the last minute of the eleventh hour. When the struggle ended a few years later, the Dutch were left in possession of the former Portuguese settlements on the Gold, Slave and Ivory coasts, but the Portuguese retained control of the slave-markets of Angola and Benguela.[3]

In Brazil, the Dutch at one time (1635–1644) occupied the northern and richer half of the colony; but the inhabitants of Pernambuco rebelled against them in June 1645. After nearly a decade of bitter warfare, the last Dutch stronghold capitulated in January 1654. The insurgents' original password was "sugar", which indicates clearly enough one of the main causes of the war, though *odium theologicum* between Calvinist and Romanist played an even more important part in the outbreak of the rebellion. Both sides used Amerindians in this struggle, as did the British and French later in Canada and North America. In fact, the bulk of the Portuguese, or rather of the Luso-Brazilian forces in this campaign consisted of Mulattoes, Negroes, Amerindians, and half-breeds of various kinds. Their most outstanding leader, João Fernandes Vieira, was the son of a Madeira *fidalgo* and a Mulata prostitute. The natural chagrin of the Dutch at the loss of north-east Brazil was greatly increased by their realization that they

[3] For details of the Luso-Dutch struggle in West Africa cf. António de Oliveira de Cadornega, *Historia geral das guerras Angolanas*, 1680 (Lisboa, 1940-42), 3 vols.; Ralph Delgado, *Historia de Angola*, Vols. 2 and 3; C. R. Boxer, *Salvador de Sá and the struggle for Brazil and Angola 1602-1686* (London, 1952); K. Ratelband, *Vijf Dagregisters van het Kasteel Elmina, 1645-1647* (The Hague, 1953).

had been defeated by what was in great part a coloured army.[4] The sugar-trade of Brazil was thus finally left in the undisputed possession of the Portuguese, after the Dutch had enjoyed a large share of it for many years. Nevertheless, the Dutch efforts were not entirely wasted as far as the sugar-industry was concerned; for improved methods of sugar cultivation and grinding were introduced into the Antilles from Pernambuco during the Dutch occupation, probably through the agency of Portuguese Jews.

The disasters which the Portuguese suffered at the hands of the Dutch during the first forty years of the seventeenth century, formed one of the chief reasons why they rebelled against the Spanish Crown in 1640; but they were disappointed in their hope that the Dutch would cease their aggression against the Portuguese *conquistas* as soon as these and the mother-country severed their connection with Spain. On the contrary, the Dutch intensified their attacks after the expiration of a ten-year Luso-Dutch truce concluded in 1641, which, incidentally, was ill-observed in Angola and Ceylon. The intensification of this colonial war led to the Portuguese seeking the protection of an English alliance, through Charles II's marriage to Dona Catarina de Bragança in 1661. The peace which Portugal subsequently secured with Spain and the United Provinces through

[4] "He ella a raiva dos Hollandezes com a guerra do Brazil ser de negros e mulatos, e mulatos e negros os que a gouvernavam; nomeavam em primeiro lugar a João Fernandes Vieira, Camaram, e Henrique Dias, e que até os dois coroneis que sam brancos, hum se chamava Martim Soares Moreno, e outro André Vidal de Negreiros; e Rei que tais negros, mulatos e morenos, e negreiros tem por vassallos, tudo hade fazer pelos conservar, quanto mais o que he virtude" (Francisco de Sousa Coutinho, Portuguese envoy at The Hague, in a dispatch dated May, 1649, in *Correspondência Diplomática de Francisco de Sousa Coutinho*, (Coimbra, 1920-55), 3 vols. Vol. III, p. 357. For details of the Luso-Dutch war in Brazil, cf. C. R. Boxer, *The Dutch in Brazil, 1624-1654* (London, 1957); J. A. Gonsalves de Mello, *João Fernandes Vieira, Mestre do campo do terço da infantaria de Pernambuco* (Recife, 1956), 2 vols.

English mediation was a peace of exhaustion as far as Portugal was concerned. The sacrifice of Bombay and Tangier to the English as part of D. Catarina's dowry was naturally resented by the Portuguese, although there was no likelihood of their being able to develop those two possessions in the existing circumstances.

The reasons for the Dutch success in Asia can be reduced to three main heads; firstly, superior economic resources, secondly, superior manpower, thirdly, superior sea power. The United Provinces, as the greatest trading nation of the seventeenth century, were vastly superior in actual and potential economic strength to the impoverished kingdom of Portugal. The population of the two countries was probably about the same ($1\frac{1}{4}$ million); but whereas Portugal had to supply cannon-fodder in the service of (or against) Spain during this period, the Dutch could and did make extensive use of German and Scandinavian manpower in their armies and fleets. The disparity in sea power was even more striking, and was expressed with only slight exaggeration by the great Portuguese Jesuit, António Vieira, in 1649. He estimated that the Dutch possessed over 14,000 vessels which could be used as warships, whereas Portugal did not possess thirteen ships of this kind. The Dutch, he claimed, had a quarter of a million sailors available, whereas Portugal had fewer than four thousand.[5]

I may add that the Dutch governor-generals at Batavia, and particularly Antonio Van Diemen, who broke the back of Portuguese sea power in the Indian Ocean during his governorship from 1636 to 1645, possessed a much better understanding of the use of sea power than did most of their 'opposite numbers', the Portuguese viceroys at Goa. Moreover, the Portuguese, with their almost exclusive reliance on *fidalgos*, or gentlemen of blood and coat-

[5] For Vieira's figures and a discussion of their reliability, cf. C. R. Boxer, *The Dutch in Brazil, 1624-1654*, pp. 204-05.

armour, as military and naval leaders, were at a disadvantage compared with the commanders in the service of the Dutch East India Company, where merit and not birth was the main criterion for promotion. This fact did not escape the more intelligent Portuguese observers. One of them, writing in 1656, pointedly contrasted the aristocratic *fidalgos* who had lost Malacca and Ceylon, with the working-class Hollanders who had conquered those places.[6]

In view of the advantages enjoyed by the Dutch, only a few of which I have enumerated here, it may be asked why they took some sixty years to conquer part of Portuguese Asia, and why they failed completely in Brazil after such a promising start? Several reasons can be suggested, but I have time to discuss only one of them now. This is, that the Portuguese, with all their faults, had struck deeper roots as colonists; and so they could not, as a rule, be removed from the scene simply by a naval or by a military defeat, or even by a series of such defeats.

Many of the Dutch were conscious of this fact, and it impressed such different observers as Governor-General Antonio van Diemen at Batavia, and Corporal Johan Saar in Ceylon. The former wrote to his superiors at Amsterdam in 1642:

Most of the Portuguese in India [=Asia] look upon this region as their father-land, and think no more about Portugal. They drive little or no trade thither, but content themselves with the interport trade of Asia, just as if they were natives thereof and had no other country.

Corporal Saar, after some years' service against the Portuguese in Ceylon, wrote of them twenty years later:

[6] "Só os fidalgos são capazes de governos altos, saibão, ou não saibão, sejão ou não sejão para a guerra. Agora governa Ceilão hum marinheiro, hum filho de hum carniceiro; outros similhantes governão Malacca; estes as ganharão, e as governarão; e os outros as governarão e as perderão" (*apud* H. Fitzler, *O Cerco de Colombo*, p. 192).

54

Wherever they once come, there they mean to settle for the rest of their lives, and they never think of returning to Portugal again. But a Hollander, when he arrives in Asia, thinks: "when my six years of service are up, then I will go home to Europe again".

Saar goes on to explain, correctly enough, that when the Dutch took Colombo, Cochin, and other well-built Portuguese settlements, they immediately dismantled much of the houses, walls, and fortifications, contenting themselves with about a third of the ground-space occupied by their predecessors.[7] *Mutatis mutandis*, similar criticisms could be applied to the temporary Dutch domination in north-eastern Brazil and along the coast of Angola and Benguela. Count Johan Maurits, whose enlightened governorship of Netherlands-Brazil is still acknowledged by many Brazilians to-day, never ceased to warn his superiors at The Hague and Amsterdam that unless they would send out Dutch, German and Scandinavian emigrants in large numbers to replace (or to mix with) the existing Portuguese settlers, the latter would always remain Portuguese at heart, and would revolt at the first opportunity.

Another reason for the greater permanence of Portuguese influence, was the wide and deep acceptance of their language, which had become a commercial lingua franca along the coasts of Africa and Asia by the time that the Dutch appeared on the scene. During the twenty-four years in which the Dutch held all or part of north-east Brazil, the Portuguese population obstinately refused to learn the language of their heretic overlords, and it is

[7] G. G. Antonio van Diemen to the Heeren XVII, October, 1642, *apud* N. MacLeod, *De Oost-Indische Compagnie als zeemogendheid in Azië, 1602-1652*, Vol. II, p. 140; *Reisbeschryving van Johan Jacobsz. Saar naar Oost-Indien, 1644-1659* (Amsterdam, 1672), p. 72. The Dutch expansion of urban Recife in Brazil is an interesting exception to this generalization.

believed that only two Dutch words have survived in the popular language of Pernambuco. In Angola and the Congo, although the Negroes rallied to the side of the Dutch for as long as their seven-year domination lasted, and although the Dutch treated the native inhabitants better than the Portuguese had done, as the latter freely admitted, yet the Negroes made no effort to learn the language of their allies and they continued to speak Portuguese. One of the Dutch Directors at Luanda observed in 1642 that if the Netherlanders wished to consolidate their position in the Congo and Angola, they must induce the Bantu to learn their language, as the Portuguese had done so successfully in their pioneer days of the sixteenth century. His advice does not seem to have been followed by his superiors, who were more interested in spreading Dutch trade than the Dutch language or culture. In the upshot, the Hollanders were not long enough in this region to put the suggested policy into practice for more than a few years. They had more success in Brazil with some of their cannibal Tapuya allies, as Padre António Vieira found on his visit to the Amerindians of the Serra de Ibiapaba in 1656, but this did not compensate for their failure to impose their own language on the Luso-Brazilian *moradores*.[8]

In Asia, the Portuguese language, or rather the Creole dialects derived therefrom, resisted Dutch official pressure and legislation with even more remarkable success. The King (or Emperor) of Ceylon, Raja Sinha II (1629–1687), though allied with the Hollanders against the Portuguese, refused to accept letters or dispatches written in Dutch, and insisted on their being in Portuguese, which language he spoke and wrote fluently. The contemporary Muslim

---

[8] Cf. the quotations from Peter Mortamer, Nicholas de Graaf, and other 17th century sources in C. R. Boxer, 'Portuguese and Dutch colonial rivalry, 1641-1661', *Studia. Revista Semestral*, Vol. 2, pp. 31-33, 1958.

regents of Macassar in Indonesia likewise spoke fluent Portuguese, and one of them had even read all the works of the Spanish devotional writer, Fray Luís de Granada O.P., in the original. In Malacca, Ceylon, Malabar, and elsewhere, some form of Portuguese patois survived into the twentieth century. and even lingers on in a few places to-day. In April 1645. Gerrit Demmer, the governor of the Moluccas, observed that Portuguese, or even English, seemed to be an easier language for the Ambonese to learn and more attractive to them than Dutch.

The most noteworthy example of the victory of the language of Camões over that of Vondel, was provided by the Dutch colonial capital of Batavia, "Queen of the Eastern Seas". The Portuguese never set foot there, save as prisoners of war, or as occasional and fleeting visitors. Yet a Creole form of their language was introduced by slaves and household servants from the region of the Bay of Bengal, and was spoken by the Dutch and half-caste women born and bred at Batavia, sometimes to the exclusion of their own mother-tongue. Governor-General Maetsuycker and his Council explained to their superiors in the Netherlands in 1659 that it was futile to try to take drastic measures against the use of Portuguese. They wrote:

The Portuguese language is an easy language to speak and easy to learn. That is the reason why we cannot prevent the slaves brought here from Arakan who have never heard a word of Portuguese (and indeed even our own children) from taking to that language in preference to all other languages and making it their own.[9]

It would be easy to multiply such quotations.

The part played by women in Portuguese colonial

[9] For the observations of Gerrit Demmer and Johann Maetsuycker on the ubiquity of the Portuguese language in Asia see K. W. Gunawardena, 'A New Netherlands in Ceylon,' *The Ceylon Journal of Historical and Social Studies*, Vol. 2, No. 2, p. 242, 1959.

Plate 4
Ruins of the 16th-century church at São Salvador do Congo
(The oldest European building in Africa South of the Equator)
A photograph taken for the author in 1955

society deserves more consideration than it receives in the standard histories, which, indeed, hardly mention women at all, other than queens and princesses. As was inevitable in the circumstances, very few women left Portugal with their menfolk for the East. One of the annual India Fleets might take 3,000 or 4,000 men to Goa, but there were seldom more than twenty or thirty women aboard, and often none at all. Even fewer went to the African colonies, whether on the east or on the west coast, and for obvious reasons, as they were notoriously places where Europeans were short-lived.

The Portuguese Crown—unlike the Spanish—tended to discourage women from going out to the Asian and African colonies, with the sole exception of the "Orphans of the King". These, as their name implies, were orphan girls of marriageable age who were sent out in batches from Lisbon at the expense of the Crown. They were provided with dowries in the form of minor government posts for anybody who would marry them. Their numbers were very limited, and it was alleged that the majority of them either died or else miscarried in childbirth. Others were

58

alleged to be virtuous enough, but too old and too ugly to find husbands. I may add that those who reached Goa safely were not necessarily married to Portuguese men. Some were given in wedlock to refugee or to vassal Asian princes, such as an exiled king of Maldives, a young prince of Mombasa, a refugee Sheikh of Pemba, and so forth, obviously with the idea of strengthening the loyalty of their husbands. But the *orfãs del Rei*, as these girls were called, were too few to make much demographical difference to the population of Portuguese Asia and Africa. The overwhelming majority of Portuguese men inevitably entered into either regular or else irregular unions—often enough, both—with Asian and Eurasian women.[10]

The Portuguese kings usually, though not invariably, favoured the policy of mixed marriages which had been initiated by Affonso de Albuquerque after his conquest of Goa in 1510. Albuquerque pointed out that a family man made a better colonist than did a gay bachelor disporting himself with his doxies. He stated that the Indians realized that the Portuguese had come to stay when they saw them planting trees, building houses, and raising families. Crown officials and Jesuit missionaries felt the same way in colonial Brazil some forty years later. One of the former wrote that a single married man was worth ten bachelors, since the latter only thought of moving on or going back home, whereas the former sought to cultivate the land and build a homestead. It was not, however, always easy to induce Portuguese men to marry, whether in Asia, Africa, or Brazil. Many of them preferred to live in concubinage with as many coloured women as they could afford to maintain—or who could afford to maintain them,

[10] For the *orfãs del Rei* (originally of the *Rainha*) see Germano da Silva Correia, *História da colonização portuguesa na Índia* (Lisboa, 1948-58), 6 vols., though this work must be used with caution as the author often ascribes a purely European origin to women who were of Eurasian or mixed blood.

in not a few instances. The universal practice of slavery also encouraged Lusitanian concupiscence on a staggering scale, and the widespread prostitution of female slaves was repeatedly denounced by the higher clergy without much lasting effect. For obvious reasons, the mortality rate among these white men was much higher than, it was among their coloured women, with the result that all the Portuguese settlements were burdened with a large surplus of widows and orphans, who were often forced to live in the depths of misery and degradation.[11]

There are, of course, exceptions to every rule, and among the white or half-caste women who became wealthy land-owners or slaveowners, or both, may be cited the *donas de Zambesia*, or heiresses of entailed estates (*prazos*) in the Zambezi river valley, and the *donas de Ibo* or ladies of Ibo in the Querimba Islands, where fortunes were made in trading for gold, ivory, and slaves with the east African continent. Theoretically, the *prazos* were supposed to be held by white women who were married to white men, the lands descending in the female line for three generations, after which they might revert to the Crown. In practice, these stipulations were seldom observed, and most of the *prazos* were owned by Mulata women whose children were apt to be of the same hue. It is generally said that this system was instituted in the eighteenth century, but a

[11] "A gente mesquinha de que abundão para sua ruina todas as nossas praças," as Padre Francisco de Sousa S.J. wrote of the siege of Mombasa, 1696-98, in his *Oriente Conquistado* (Lisboa, 1710), 2 vols. Vol. II, pp. 53-54. For similar remarks about the Portuguese in Cochim see João Ribeiro, *Fatalidade Historica da Ilha de Ceilão*, *1685*, Livro III, cap. 3, and cap. 8 ("aonde só achárão os Hollandezes, quando renderão esta cidade mais de dez mil mulheres brancas [*sic*] desobrigadas, sem pais, nem maridos"). Cf. also Alexander Hamilton's observations on the superfluity of women in Macau in his *New Account of East India, 1727*, ed. W. Foster (London, 1930), 2 vols., Vol. II, p. 116. When the Portuguese governor evacuated Lifao in 1769 and transferred the headquarters of the Portuguese in Timor to Dili, the majority of the 1,200 evacuees were women and girls.

Jesuit account of Zambesia in 1667 shows that it was already in existence in an embryo form at that date.[12]

Whatever the drawbacks of miscegenation as practised by the Portuguese, the offspring of these unions, whether legitimate or otherwise, did remain loyal to the Portuguese Crown and to the Roman Catholic religion, often for long after the Portuguese themselves had gone. It was also mainly through the half-caste and native women that the Portuguese adopted or adapted so many Asian, African and Amerindian habits or usages, in such things as household management, cooking, and modifications of dress and diet. It was the Eurasian and the half-caste, or even the slave women, who kept alive the use of the Portuguese language in places like Batavia, Malacca, and Ceylon, which were under Dutch control, as I indicated previously.

Portuguese women were notoriously the most secluded in Europe, and it was the boast of a seventeenth-century Portuguese writer that a virtuous Portuguese woman left her house only for her christening, her marriage, and her funeral. This, incidentally, reminds one of the similar Japanese proverb that a woman has three successive lords during her life-time—her father when she is a child, her husband when she is married, and her son if she becomes a widow. This seclusion of Portuguese women, whether derived from the Moorish domination of the Iberian peninsula or not, at any rate helped to accustom the Portuguese to the harem- and zenana-like seclusion imposed on women in most countries of the East. It is amusing to note the Dutch reactions to this practice. They were very scornful of it during their occupation of north-east Brazil, and the freedom which they accorded to their own women horrified the contemporary Luso-Brazilian men.

[12] Padre Manuel Barreto S.J., cited by Conego Alcantara Guerreiro, 'Quadros Historicos de Moçambique', *Mocambique. Documentario Trimestral*, No. 66, p.43, 1951.

Fr. Manuel Calado, who has left us a fascinating account of life in occupied Pernambuco in his *Valeroso Lucideno*, tells us that from 1630 to 1647 there was not a single instance of a Portuguese man marrying a Dutch woman, or even, he adds slyly, of having a love-affair with one. On the other hand, there were a number of instances of Dutch men espousing Luso-Brazilian women, and in most of these cases the men tended subsequently to adopt their wives' country and religion. Similar mixed marriages took place in the East, though the Dutch authorities were inclined to regard them askance, principally because the children and even the husbands likewise tended to become Roman Catholics. Governor-General Johan Maetsuycker (1653–1678), while aware of this danger, and of the allegedly immoral tendencies of half-caste women, was a great admirer of the Portuguese system of secluding their wives, which he held up as an example for the Dutch colonists to follow. He suggested that all Eurasian women married to Dutch husbands should be kept confined to their houses, though he did not explain how this was to be done.[13]

Another factor which helped to perpetuate Portuguese influence, even in places which remained under Dutch domination for centuries, was religion. Although, as I stated in my last lecture, Portuguese methods of propagating their faith were sometimes more coercive than persuasive, and although they achieved no success whatever against Islam, and made only a relatively slight impression in India and in China, yet where they did succeed in implanting Roman Catholicism, it usually took deep root. An instance

[13] For Maetsuycker's praise of the Portuguese habit of secluding their women see K. W. Gunawardena, 'A New Netherlands in Ceylon,' pp. 212-13, 238. The whole of this article is worth reading for its account of the part played by Indo-Portuguese women in Dutch territory. For the situation in Netherlands Brazil cf. C. R. Boxer, *The Dutch in Brazil*, 1624-1654, pp. 125-30, and J. A. Gonsalves de Mello, *Tempo dos Flamengos* (Rio de Janeiro 1947) pp. 166-69.

of this is provided by the futile efforts of the Dutch to eradicate it in the Asian settlements which they took from the Portuguese—Amboina alone excepted. These efforts lasted intermittently for a century and a half, but during all that time the Calvinist *predikant* could never compete on equal terms with the Roman Catholic priest. The Eurasian communities of Batavia, Malacca, Coromandel, Ceylon and Malabar, whenever they had the chance, and often at considerable risk to themselves, would leave the Protestant preacher to hear mass said, or to have their children baptized, or their marriages solemnized by some passing Roman Catholic priest in disguise.[14] With a few exceptions, the Calvinist converts made by the Dutch have left no trace at the present day, whereas the Roman Catholic communities planted by the Portuguese are still flourishing in many places.

I said in my first lecture that the Portuguese colonial empire was a commercial and maritime organization cast in a military and clerical mould. The cross and the sword; God and Mammon; Christians and spices (or, in the case of Brazil, sugar)—all these factors were constantly, and often incongruously, involved. As Diogo do Couto, a Portuguese

---

[14] "Consentem em Malacca misquitas de Mouros, e pagodes de gentios; e perguntando hum de nossos padres a hum seu Domine porque não consentião tambem igreja de Càtholicos, respondeo muito desabafado, que se a ouvesse, tambem os seus a frequentarião" (Fernão de Queiroz S.J., *Conquista Temporal e espiritual de Ceylão*, (1916), p. 971). Cf. F. de Haan, *Oud Batavia*, Vol. I, p. 518, apropos of the Mardijckers of Batavia: "Verscheen er een Roomsche pater in de stad, dan liepen zij bij hoopen van de preek naar de mis," and ibid., p. 122. Antonio Van Diemen had acknowledged regretfully in 1631 that the Portuguese Roman Catholic missionaries were much more zealous and successful than were their Calvinist rivals ("in datt stuck zijn se ons te cloeck ende bethoonen hare papen veel meer ijver ende neersticheijtt, als well onse leeraers ende predicanten." Cf. W. P. Coolhaas, 'Een Indisch verslag uit 1631, van de hand van Antonio van Diemen' in *Bijdragen en Mededelingen der Historisch Genootschap te Utrecht*, Vol. 65, p. 41, 1943-46.

soldier-chronicler who spent most of his life in India, wrote in 1612:

> The Kings of Portugal always aimed in their conquest of the East at so uniting the two powers, spiritual and temporal, that the one should never be exercised without the other.

This indissoluble union of the Cross and the Crown was exemplified in the exercise of the *Padroado Real*, or Royal Patronage of the Church, whose long and stormy history in the struggle for souls was concerned not only with Muslims, Gentiles and heretics, but with the missionaries of other Roman Catholic powers.

The Portuguese *Padroado* can be loosely defined as a combination of the rights and duties inherited by the Crown of Portugal as patron of the Roman Catholic missions and ecclesiastical establishments in a large part of Africa, in Asia, and in Brazil. In fact, the Portuguese *Padroado Real* in the non-European world was originally only limited by the similar Papal privileges conferred on the Castilian kings' *Patronato Real* in Spanish America and the Philippines. The Renaissance Popes, owing to their preoccupation with European politics, with the rising tide of Protestantism, and with the Turkish threat to Italy, did not concern themselves very closely with the evangelization of the new worlds opened by the Portuguese and Spanish discoveries. Those Popes saw no harm in letting the Iberian monarchs bear the expense of building chapels and churches, maintaining a religious hierarchy, and sending missionaries to convert the heathen, in exchange for granting those rulers extensive privileges in the way of presenting bishops to vacant sees, collecting tithes, and administering ecclesiastical taxation. In the case of Portugal, the kings received these privileges not in their capacity as crowned heads, but as administrators, governors, and, finally, Grand Masters of the Order of Christ. This was a military-religious Order founded by King Dom Dinis in 1319, to replace the recently suppressed Order of the Templars. It was incorporated in the Crown in 1551, and given the superintendance of all the overseas missions in the Portuguese colonial world by the sixteenth century papacy.[15]

By the mid-seventeenth century, the situation had changed considerably. The papacy then found that the extensive privileges, amounting to a monopoly of church patronage, which had been so freely bestowed on the Crowns of Spain and Portugal in the previous two centuries were in many respects highly inconvenient and subversive of papal authority. There was nothing much that the Popes could do about the Spanish-American empire, where the Castilian kings' *Patronato Real* was maintained virtually intact down to the independence of Spanish America in the early nineteenth century. But the Portuguese were in a much weaker position after their monopoly of the Asian and African seas had been broken by the Dutch and the English. The papacy was therefore enabled to whittle down and pare away the claims of the Portuguese *Padroado Real* in both Asia and Africa throughout the seventeenth and eighteenth centuries. This increasing papal control was exercised primarily through the Sacred College of the Propaganda Fide, founded at Rome in 1622, and secondarily through encouraging the establishment of French and Italian missions in Africa and the East. In Brazil it was another story. The Portuguese position on the other side of the Atlantic was as strong as that of the Spaniards in the rest of Latin America, and the papacy was constrained to

[15] A. da Silva Rego, *O padroado Português do Oriente. Esboço histórico* (Lisboa, 1940); C-M de Witte, *Les Bulles Pontificales et l'expansion Portugaise au XVe siécle* (Louvain, 1958) and the articles of António Brásio in *Studia. Revista Semestral* Vol. 2, pp. 313-18, 1958 and Vol. 3, pp. 124-54, 1959.

admit the full functioning of the Portuguese *Padroado* in Brazil until that country achieved her independence. Portuguese pride strongly resented this attitude of successive popes, and the Portuguese kings fought a rear-guard action in defence of their cherished *Padroado* rights which lasted for over three centuries. This struggle had many repercussions in India, Indochina, China and elsewhere, which I have not time to discuss now. Suffice it to say, that the last vestiges of the Portuguese *Padroado* in India (outside of the Portuguese possessions) was only abandoned by Portugal a few years ago, after diplomatic pressure by Mr Nehru's government. [16]

The spearhead of the Portuguese missions, and often (though not always) of the *Padroado* was formed by the Company (or Society) of Jesus, from shortly after its inauguration in 1540 until its suppression by Pombal in 1760. During this period of almost exactly two centuries, the Jesuits were to the fore as missionaries and as martyrs from Brazil to Japan. They were also conspicuous as the educators of colonial youth, and their numerous colleges were the principal centres of culture throughout the Portuguese-speaking world. Both as missionaries and as educators, they set and maintained, in general, much higher standards then did the friars of the Mendicant Orders—Dominicans, Franciscans, Augustinians and Carmelites—with whom they were often on anything but friendly terms. As they were also the best and the most respected teachers of the Portuguese aristocracy in the mother country, and as they frequently supplied confessors to successive Portuguese kings, their prestige, power, and

---

[16] P. A. Jann O Min.Cap., *Die katholischen missionen und das Portu-giesische Patronat vom 15 bis ins 18 jahrhundert* (Paderborn, 1915); A. da Silva Rego, *O padroado Português do Oriente* (Lisboa, 1940); ibid. *Curso de missionologia* (Lisboa, 1956), pp. 115-70; H. Chappoulie, *Rome et les missions d'Indochine au xviie siécle* (Paris, 1943-48), 2 vols.

influence were correspondingly great. *Vice-rei vá, vice-rei vem, Padre Paulista sempre tem*—"Viceroys come and viceroys go, but the Jesuit Fathers are always with us"— was a proverbial expression among the inhabitants of Goa.

To maintain the missions, the Jesuits perforce engaged in trade on a considerable scale, as indeed did many of the friars and clergy in places like East Africa, where clerical stipends were paid in trade-goods, such as cotton textiles, and not in money. The Jesuits were also large property-holders everywhere, including sugar plantations and cattle ranches in Brazil, agricultural estates in Angola, and villages of palm groves in India. The wealth which they derived from these land-holdings, and from the commerce which they drove in many places, was naturally the topic of much malicious gossip and of severe criticism. Some of the latter was certainly justified at certain times and places, as, for example in Angola during the years 1659–1662, though the other religious Orders were by no means immune from similar charges, as instanced by the Dominicans in eighteenth-century Zambesia. But on the whole, Protestant Peter Mundy was right when he declared in 1638, after seeing something of the Jesuits' missionary and educational work in the East: "And to speak truly, they spare neither cost nor labour, diligence nor danger, to attain their purpose"—the greater glory of God. In other words, they certainly made good money, but they certainly spent it on good works.[17]

Another feature of the Jesuits' activities which aroused great opposition was their struggle for the freedom of the

---

[17] C. R. Boxer, *Fidalgos in the Far East, 1550-1770* (The Hague, 1948), pp. 157-73. For João Fernandes Vieira's criticism of the Jesuits in Angola 1659-1662, and a discussion as to how far it was justified cf. Francisco Rodrigues S.J., *Historia da Companhia de Jesus na Assistência de Portugal* (Porto, 1931-44), 6 vols., Vol. III (2), pp. 293-99; Ralph Delgado, *Historia de Angola*, Vol. III, pp. 232-38; J. A. Gonsalves de Mello, *João Fernandes Vieira*, Vol. II, pp. 185-91.

Amerindians in Brazil. The Jesuits alone among the religious Orders in Brazil, had a long tradition of upholding the freedom of the Amerindians against all the efforts of the colonists to enslave and exploit them, although the Capuchins also took a similar stand at certain times and places. The Jesuits' most famous spokesman, Padre António Vieira, whose life roughly coincided with the seventeenth century, asserted that Portuguese mistreatment of the Amerindians had resulted in the deaths of over two million of them during forty years in the Amazon region alone. His exaggerations in this respect recall those of his sixteenth-century Spanish precursor, the Dominican friar Bartolomé de Las Casas. Unlike Las Casas, however, Vieira and the great majority of his Portuguese colleagues did not see anything inherently wrong in the enslavement of Negroes, as opposed to that of Amerindians. But the missionaries did protest with fair frequency against the cruel treatment to which African slaves were often subjected in the Brazilian sugar plantations, where the average life of a slave was estimated at seven years.

In the struggle between the Jesuits and the colonists over the freedom of the Amerindians, the Crown of Portugal pursued a somewhat vacillating course, although its intervention was usually effected on the side of the Jesuits. The laws which were successively framed at Lisbon to protect the interests of the Amerindians were thus mostly of a compromise character which satisfied neither party to the dispute. But the Jesuits' attitude and particularly the influence of António Vieira, who for many years was one of the Crown's leading advisers, did protect the Brazilian Indians from some of the worst excesses which their brethren suffered in Spanish America. The Jesuits' condemnation of the mistreatment of African slaves can be seen from two eighteenth-century works published by members of the Society which deal with Negro slavery in whole or in part.[18] Their pleas on behalf of this oppressed race were not quite so eloquent as those of their seventeenth-century Spanish-American forerunner, Alonso de Sandoval S.J.. whose *Naturaleza, policia sagrada i profana, costumbres i ritos de todos Etiopes*, published at Seville in 1627, anticipated many of the arguments of the Anglo-Saxon abolitionists.

The seventeenth-century years of crisis witnessed several major changes in the position of Portugal's empire. The most important of these changes were the declining importance of her Oriental possessions and the growing importance of Brazil and Angola. The reverses suffered by the Portuguese during the sixty-years struggle with the Dutch in Asia had encouraged others to attack their enfeebled empire in the East. By the end of the century, the Arabs of Oman had developed into a sea power which not only harassed the Portuguese in the Persian Gulf and on the west coast of India, but took Mombasa from them and threatened Moçambique. Portuguese efforts to deal with the rise of the Omani were handicapped by the growth of the Maratha power in India which gave them plenty of anxiety nearer Goa. These constant wars and the resulting economic decay meant that the *fumos da India* no longer held the attractions that they did when *Goa Dourada* was in its prime and rivalled Lisbon in importance.

As early as 1645, a Portuguese who knew Brazil well wrote that:

Portugal has no other region more fertile. nor closer at hand nor more frequented, nor have its vassals a

[18] João Antonil (*alias* Andreoni) S.J., *Cultura e opulencia do Brasil* (Lisboa, 1711), Parte I, cap. ix; Jorge Benci S.J., *Economia cristã dos senhores no governo dos escravos* (Rome, 1705; reprinted, Porto, 1954); Manuel Ribeiro Rocha, *Ethiope Resgatado, empenhado, sustentado* (Lisboa, 1758). For Vieira's defence of the freedom of the Amerindians cf. the volume entitled *Em defesa dos Indios* in the series *Obras Escolhidas* edited by A. Sergio and H. Cidade (Lisboa, 1951-54), 12 vols.

better and a safer refuge than Brazil. The Portuguese who is overtaken by any misfortune at home, emigrates thither.[19]

This was written at a time when nearly half of the country was under Dutch control; and after the expulsion of the heretic invaders and the revival of the sugar trade ten years later, emigration naturally increased still more. By the sixteen-eighties about 2,000 men were emigrating yearly from Portugal to Brazil, and the overwhelming majority went voluntarily. The ships sailing to India, on the other hand, by this time carried only exiles, convicts, and jail-birds conscripted as soldiers, and their annual total did not often exceed a thousand. White women did not emigrate to Brazil in large numbers, but at any rate many more made this relatively short and easy voyage than embarked on the long and dangerous passage to India.

King François I of France had, it may be recalled, somewhat unkindly termed Dom Manuel I, "Le Roi Epicier", the "Grocer King". A hundred and fifty years later this epithet was no longer quite so applicable to the reigning Portuguese monarch, D. João IV, who might, however, have been fairly called the "Sugar King". He himself referred to Brazil as his *vacca de leite*, or milch-cow; and it was the resources supplied by Brazilian sugar, tobacco, dyewoods and other tropical products, which enabled Portugal to pay the armies which defended her frontier against Spain, and to secure the support of France and Great Britain.

[19] Gaspar Ferreira to D. João IV, The Hague, 20 July 1645 *Revista do Instituto Archeologico e geographico Pernambucauo*, No. 32, p. 78, 1887.

70

IV

THE GOLDEN AGE OF BRAZIL IN THE EIGHTEENTH CENTURY

Portuguese colonization of Brazil, which began in a serious way in the fifteen-thirties, was for long confined to a narrow coastal strip. Even the littoral was adequately colonized only in a few regions, and the settled area did not, with one exception, extend for more than about thirty miles inland. Sugar, later supplemented by tobacco, formed the staple export, and in view of the total absence of roads and the modest length of the navigable rivers, the sugar plantations had to be situated within easy reach of a harbour. Pernambuco in the north, Bahia in the centre, and Rio de Janeiro in the south, were the three chief centres of sugar production and consequently of population. The slave labour for the plantations and households of the colonists was drawn mainly from west Africa, originally from Guinea, and, after the foundation of Luanda in 1575, increasingly from Angola and Benguela. The colonists also enslaved Amerindians for the same purpose; but as the aborigines were still in the Stone Age stage of civilization, they did not prove so useful or so resistant to disease as the Negroes.

Penetration of the interior began relatively early in the extreme south, where the inhabitants of the highland plateau of São Paulo, being too poor to buy Negro slaves, raided deep into the hinterland, in search of Amerindians to enslave for labour in their farms and homes. They even penetrated as far as the Cordillera of the Andes to the west and to the Amazon on the north; but these were slave-raiding expeditions which left no settlements in the country which they traversed. The Paulistas had a high percentage of Amerindian blood in their veins, and they often spoke Tupi among themselves in preference to Portuguese. They adopted, or adapted, many of the customs and techniques of the savages with whom they mixed so freely, resembling in this as in other respects the French-Canadian *métis* or *coureurs du bois* of the seventeenth century.

Less spectacular, but more effective in the long run was the more gradual advance of the *vaqueiros*, cowboys or stockmen, particularly in the second half of the seventeenth century after the end of the Dutch wars. In search of grazing lands for their cattle, these men, mainly half-breeds in the employ of latifundian landowners, gradually pushed westwards from Bahia and Pernambuco. They successively opened up in this way the backlands of the north-east, and the region of the São Francisco river valley in the centre. In their case, this advance was accompanied by occupation, though naturally the population was very thin on the ground, being confined to the sparsely-manned ranches.

By the last quarter of the seventeenth century, Portugal depended chiefly on its exports of sugar, tobacco, wine, fruit and salt, to pay for its essential imports of cereals and of manufactured goods. The value of these exports never sufficed to pay for the imports, and the country's balance of payments problem became increasingly critical. In 1671 the experienced English consul at Lisbon, Thomas Maynard, reported:

All their sugars which are arrived this year, with all other commodities this kingdom affords to be exported, will not pay for half of the goods that are imported, so that their money will all be carried out of their kingdom within a few years.

The economic outlook was equally gloomy on the other side

of the Atlantic, where the Jesuit Padre António Vieira wrote from Bahia in 1689:

We shall shortly relapse into the savage state of the Indians, and become Brazilians instead of Portuguese.[1]

Perhaps things were never quite so bad as both foreign and Portuguese observers thought; but in any case, just when they seemed to be at their worst, the situation was providentially eased by two factors; the Williamite wars between England and France, and the (largely accidental) discovery of gold in Brazil. King William's wars with France led to the importation of French wines into England being either prohibited altogether or else subjected to very heavy duties. This in turn led to an increased consumption of Portuguese wines in the English market, a fact which helped to redress Portugal's unfavourable balance of trade, and which was consolidated by the famous Methuen commercial treaty of 1703. As regards Brazilian gold, this was discovered in the mid-sixteen-nineties for the first time on a really large scale, by bands of Paulista adventurers. They were roving in the bush and forest country of what is now Minas Gerais, looking rather for Amerindians and for silver—which metal the Spanish had found in such dazzling quantities in Mexico and Peru—than for gold.

By the end of the seventeenth century even those who had been sceptical of the news that the yellow metal had been found in the distant hinterland north of Rio de Janeiro, had come to realize that there was indeed "gold in them thar hills" on an unprecedented scale. New and rich workings were discovered almost daily over a wide area,

[1] Thomas Maynard's dispatch, d. Lisbon, 9 December 1671 (Public Record Office, London, SP 89/11, fl. 283); António Vieira S.J., to Diogo Marchão Temudo, Bahia, 13 July 1689, in J. L. Azevedo, *Cartas de António Vieira* (Coimbra, 1925-28), Vol. 3, p. 581, '...brevemente tornaremos ao primitivo estado dos Indios, e os Portugueses seremos Brasis."

where every river, brook, and stream seemed to contain gold. The gold, I may add, was all of the alluvial or placer variety. A good many years elapsed before underground mining for gold was attempted, and then only in a few places and on a relatively limited scale. The gold mines were really more in the nature of washings or of diggings; though the region where the gold was found was soon given the name, which it still retains, of Minas Gerais or the General Mines.

Inevitably, the Paulista discoverers and pioneers were not left long in unchallenged possession of the gold diggings. A swarm of adventurers from all over the colony and from Portugal itself converged on the region by the only three practicable trails through the wilderness, leading respectively from Bahia, Rio de Janeiro, and São Paulo. "Vagabond and disorderly people, for the most part base and immoral", as the Governor-General of Brazil unflatteringly described them in 1701.[2] A less prejudiced eyewitness of this, the first great gold-rush of modern times, described it as follows:

Each year a crowd of Portuguese and of foreigners come out in the [annual] fleets in order to go to the mines. From the cities, towns, plantations and backlands of Brazil, come Whites, Coloured, and Blacks, together with many Amerindians enslaved by the Paulistas. The mixture is of all sorts and conditions of persons: men and women; young and old; rich and poor; nobles and commoners; laymen, clergy, and Religious of different Orders, many of which have neither house nor convent in Brazil.[3]

[2] ". . . gente vaga e tumultuaria, pella mayor parte gente vil e pouca morigerada" (D. João de Lencastre to the Crown, Bahia, 12 January 1701, in V. Rau, *Catálogo dos manuscritos da Casa Cadaval respeitantes ao Brasil*, (Lisboa, 1955-58), 2 vols., Vol. II, p. 15).

[3] André João Antonil [João António Andreoni], *Cultura e opulencia do Brasil* (Lisboa, 1711), Part 3, ch. 5.

The hardships endured on the trails to the mines proved too much for many of the tenderfoots, and there were numerous deaths from starvation and malnutrition among the adventurers who set out with nothing more than a stick in their hand and a knapsack on their back. No effective government control was exercised over the early pioneers once they had reached the mining region. The government officials and consequently their effective jurisdiction were still virtually confined to the coastal settlements formed near the sugar plantations.

The senior colonial officials at first regarded this gold-rush with mixed feelings. The Governor-General at Bahia, from whose dispatch of the 12 January 1701 I have just quoted, rejoiced that the latest news from the mines formed a singularly auspicious opening to the new century and gave promise of great wealth and prosperity to the mother country. Nevertheless, he added, there was a grave risk that Brazilian gold would ultimately be of no more use to Portugal than Mexican and Peruvian silver had been to Spain. Gold, on entering the Tagus, might leave the same river soon afterwards to pay for imports from England, France, Holland and Italy, "so that", he wrote, "these countries will have all the profit and we will have all the work". In point of fact, something rather like this did happen; for it may be roughly estimated that between half and three-quarters of the amount of Brazilian gold which reached Lisbon in an averagely good year—38,400 lb. avoirdupois in 1733 — left it again to pay for Portuguese imports from northern Europe, of which England supplied the lion's share.

The unruly crowds which poured into the gold diggings of Minas Gerais in the confident hope of making their fortunes there, speedily divided into two mutually hostile groups. The first comprised the original Paulista pioneers and their Amerindian slaves. The second comprised the newcomers from Portugal and from other parts of Brazil, together with their slaves, who were principally of west African origin. What amounted to a civil war between these two rival groups broke out in 1709, and after a few weeks of not very deadly fighting, culminated in the complete victory of the *Emboabas* as the newcomers were called.[4] Henceforth the white population of Minas Gerais was of predominantly Portuguese origin; but the west African slaves were even more numerous, and a large Mulatto population speedily developed from the concubinage of the miners with the Negresses.

The "War of the *Emboabas*" as the disturbances of 1709 were called, enabled the Crown to exert its authority over the turbulent mining community for the first time. Both sides had appealed to Lisbon for support, and this gave the Crown the chance to send out a governor and to create a skeleton administration in Minas Gerais. The Paulistas who had been expelled from this region by the victorious *Emboabas*, trekked westwards and discovered successively the gold-fields of Cuiabá, Goiás, and Mato Grosso. During the seventeen-twenties, diamonds were also discovered in Minas Gerais, and in 1740 the Diamond District was placed under a specially strict Crown régime. This régime virtually isolated the Diamond District from the rest of Brazil, and it could only be entered or left by persons holding written permits from the Intendant in charge.

The discovery of gold and diamonds on such a scale

[4] *Emboaba*, apparently a Tupí word for a "gaitered" or feather-legged bird; applied by the Paulistas, who habitually went bare-legged and bare-footed in the bush, to the "tenderfoots" newcomers from Europe and the coastal towns, who wore shoes and leggings of hides or bark. "Os Reynões, chamados pelos Paulistas embuabas [*sic*] por desprezo, que na sua lingua quer dizer galinhas calsadas, o que imitavão pelos calções que uzavão de rolos" (anonymous account by an 18th-century Portuguese pioneer in the São Paulo Municipal Library, Codice Costa Matoso, fl. 37).

had several major repercussions in the Portuguese colonial world. In the first place, and for the first time, it led to a large shift of population from the coastal region to the interior of Brazil. This movement was not like the slow and steady penetration previously effected in some regions by the cattle rangers, but was an emigration *en masse*. Secondly, it led to a severe and prolonged economic crisis, resulting partly from the scarcity of labour, which left the sugar and tobacco plantations and the coastal towns to seek more remunerative (it was hoped) employment in the gold-fields; and partly from a sharp rise in prices which was the unavoidable result of a labour shortage coupled with the increased production of gold. Thirdly, the increased demand for west African slaves for service in the mines and plantations of Brazil led to a corresponding increase in the slave-trade with west Africa.

Angola and Benguela proving inadequate as a source of supply, the Portuguese (or, rather, the Luso-Brazilian) slave-traders turned their attention again to the slave-markets of Guinea, whence they had been driven by the Dutch in the preceding century. Here they succeeded, though only with difficulty and against continual Dutch (and sometimes English) interference in establishing a lucrative slave-trade with the kingdom of Dahomey. It was from this region that they secured the Sudanese slaves who proved to be tougher and better fitted for work in the mines than the Bantu from Angola. And not only for work in the mines, I may add. As the governor of Rio de Janeiro reported to the Crown in July 1726: "There is not a white Miner who can live without at least one Negress from Dahomey, for they say that only with them do they have any luck."[5] A French visitor to Bahia eight years

[5] Luis Vahia Monteiro to the Crown, Rio de Janeiro, 5 July 1726, *apud* Mafaldo P. Zemella, *O Abastecimento da capitania das Minas Gerais no século XVIII* (São Paulo, 1951), p. 203.

earlier noted that even when a Portuguese man could get a white woman to wife, he often preferred to live with a woman—or women—of African blood.[6] *É a mulata que é mulher*, as the Brazilian saying goes; and this trait was likewise observed by many subsequent foreign visitors to and residents in Brazil. This sexual preference for Mulatas was not reflected in the colonial laws, which still discriminated against persons of African blood, as I shall have occasion to mention later. But these colour-bar laws were often evaded or surmounted, and as early as the mid-seventeenth century Brazil was already characterized as being "A Hell for Blacks; a Purgatory for Whites, and a Paradise for Mulattoes".[7]

The westward expansion of Brazil in the first half of the eighteenth century led to a renewal of boundary disputes with Spanish America, particularly in the upper Amazon and the lower Rio de la Plata regions. These disputes were settled by mutual concessions and exchanges of territory in a Treaty concluded at Madrid in 1750. This was the last year of the reign of Dom João V, who had astonished Europe by the prodigality with which he distributed the income which he received from Brazilian gold and diamonds. It is true that this treaty was soon denounced by the Spaniards, and that further fighting between the two powers in South America subsequently ensued. But it formed the basis of the final settlement which was reached in the

6 "Les Portugais naturels du Bresil préferent la possession d'une femme noire ou mulatre, à la plus belle femme [blanche]," Le Gentil de la Barbinnais, *Nouveau voyage autour du monde* (Paris, 1728), 3 vols., Vol. III, p. 204.

7 "Inferno dos Negros, Purgatorio dos Brancos, e Paraizo dos Mulatos, e das Mulatas," wrote Antonil (*Cultura e opulencia*, Book 1, ch. 9) in 1711, echoing with a slight difference Dom Francisco Manuel de Mello's sixty-years' earlier MS. work, "Descripção do Brazil intitulada Paraiso de Mulatos, Purgatorio dos Brancos, e Inferno dos Negros."

78

treaty of San Ildefonso twenty-seven years later, and which gave Brazil roughly her present boundaries.[8]

The spectacular development of Brazil during the reign of Dom João V was not accompanied by any lasting improvement in the condition of Portugal's Asian and African colonies, but rather the reverse. This was to a great extent unavoidable, as Portugal, whose population between 1650 and 1750 probably increased to something between two and a quarter and two and a half million, simply did not have the demographic and economic resources to develop her colonies both East and West. The decline of the African colonies was, however, accentuated by their being regarded almost exclusively as slaving depots, with the result that their agricultural and industrial needs were either ignored altogether, or else subordinated to the requirements of the slave-trade with all the demoralizing consequences which that implied. The Marquis of Castello-Novo in 1744 drew a striking contrast between the backwardness and inertia of the colony of Moçambique and the thriving development of the French islands of France and Bourbon under the enterprising government of Mahé de la Bourdonnais.[9] Angola experienced better days under the singularly enlightened rule of Francisco Innocencio de Sousa Coutinho (1764–1772) but the improvement was not maintained.

The decline of the Portuguese power in Asia was hastened by the progress of the Marathas, who conquered the "Province of the North" from them after a hard-fought campaign in 1737–40. This province comprised the Portuguese settlements along the sixty-six mile stretch of

[8] Jaime Cortesão, *Alexandre de Gusmão e o tratado de Madrid* (Rio de Janeiro, 1950-56), 7 vols., for the antecedents, negotiations, and repercussions of the treaty of 1750.
[9] Marquis of Castello-Novo to the Secretary of State, Moçambique, 22 August 1744, in the *Arquivo das Colonias* (Lisboa, 1918), Vol. III, pp. 233-40.

coast between Bombay and Damão. It was the most productive part of what Indian territory was left to them after their disasterous wars with the Dutch and with the Arabs of Oman in the preceding century. Thenceforward, the isolated settlements of Goa, Damão and Diu, on the west coast of India, Macau in China, and part of the island of Timor in the East Indies were all that remained of the once-proud State of India, after Moçambique had been made a separate government in 1752.

Despite the reverses in Asia and the stagnation in Africa, the reign of Dom João V seemed a golden age to many of his contemporaries, thanks to the wealth which he derived, or was believed to derive, from Brazil. John Wesley wrote in 1755:

> Merchants who have lived in Portugal inform us, that the King had a large building filled with diamonds; and more gold stored up, coined and uncoined, than all the other princes of Europe together.

This, of course, was not true. Portuguese gold coins were more common in the West Country of England, than they were in Portugal itself. But Wesley's observation does reflect the prevailing tendency to mistake the glitter of Dom João V's reign for the gold.[10]

The reign of the next king, Dom José I, virtually coincided with what may be fairly termed the dictatorship of the Marquis of Pombal (1755–1777). The repercussions of his rule are felt in Portugal to this day, but I have only time now briefly to consider four principal aspects of his colonial policy. These may be defined as (i) strengthening still further the extensive power of the Crown over all ramifications of colonial life; (ii) his efforts to foster colonial trade by founding privileged and monopolistic

[10] John Wesley, *Serious thoughts occasioned by the great earthquake at Lisbon* (London, 1755).

chartered trading companies; (iii) his abolition, or at least weakening of the colour-bar; (iv) his suppression of the Society of Jesus in the Portuguese empire.

Pombal's efforts to strengthen the power of the Crown merely intensified an existing state of affairs. Unlike the case with English overseas expansion, the Crown of Portugal had always taken a leading and direct share in fostering the discoveries and conquests made by its vassals. In the final analysis, everything depended, in theory at any rate, and often enough in practice, upon the personal decision of the king. Pathetic petitions by obscure widows in the backlands of Brazil, in the fever-stricken valley of the Zambezi, or in the slums of Macau; the issue of a copper coinage for Angola; the terms of a whaling contract at Bahia; the treatment of Indian Nautch girls at Goa; the activities of gold and diamond smugglers in Minas Gerais; the ecclesiastical complications of the Chinese Rites at Macau and Peking; the promotion of officers and N.C.O.'s in colonial garrisons—all these alike were grist to the Crown's mill, and all final decisions concerning them had to be made by the king himself. Since Pombal insisted on handling in the king's name these and a thousand other matters, it is not surprising that the Portuguese bureaucratic machine became more than ever clogged. Decisions on such matters often involved delays of anything from two to ten years, and many papers submitted for the royal perusal and decision were never answered at all.[11]

As regards Pombal's efforts to revive Portuguese colonial trade and commerce, these met with varying success. The Portuguese governments had often tried to

---

[11] This bureaucratic delay was not, of course, peculiar to Portugal. Stamford Raffles, the English governor of Java from 1811 to 1816, found after his return to England that some of his official dispatches were still lying in the India Office with their seals unbroken (*A narrative of the early life and services of Captain D. Macdonald, I.N.*, 3 ed. (Weymouth, [1840?] p. 239).

emulate the success of the Dutch and English East India Companies by founding similar organizations of their own, whether for the East India trade, or for the west African slave-trade, or for the Brazil trade. None of these had proved a commercial success, and they were all either still-born or short-lived, with the exception of the Brazil Company founded in 1649. This lasted in one form or another down to 1720, but it only paid two or three annual dividends during those seventy-one years. Pombal, who had begun his diplomatic career in the late seventeen-thirties as envoy to the Court of St James, where he had been greatly impressed by the apparent prosperity of the English East India Company, founded a number of state-aided and monopolistic trading companies during his dictatorship. Most of these were failures, but his Douro Wine Company and two of his Brazilian Companies (Maranhão-Pará, and Pernambuco-Paraíba) were commercial successes, at any rate for some twenty or thirty years. He also instituted the *Real Erario*, or Royal Fisc, which secured for the Crown a more systematic and far-reaching control of its revenues in Brazil. But owing to the extremely low pay of the great majority of the colonial officials, smuggling still continued on a lavish scale, and contraband trade in any given colony was often more important than the legal variety.

As regards the colour-bar, Pombal's decrees in some ways anticipated the "Liberty, Equality and Fraternity" slogan of the French Revolution. He abolished slavery in Portugal itself—admittedly largely because it was regarded askance in France and England. He promulgated the most drastic decree ordaining that the Asian subjects of the Portuguese Crown should be given the same status as white persons who were born in Portugal, on the grounds that "His Majesty does not distinguish between his vassals by their colour, but by their merits". Similar decrees were not promulgated in respect of the African colonies, as the Negroes were still regarded as being basically inferior; but in regard to the Amerindians of Brazil, Pombal went even further. He not only abolished (on paper) the last vestiges of forced labour, but he earnestly encouraged Portuguese settlers of both sexes to intermarry with the Amerindians, regardless of the latter's extremely primitive culture.

Pombal's efforts to smash the colour-bar in India and Brazil (Negroes excepted) were only partially successful. They were not welcomed by most colonial governors and high officials; and though these men did not venture to oppose the ruthless dictator during his lifetime, things soon reverted to the *status quo ante* after his death. This meant that coloured officers of Asian or Eurasian origin could never get promotion above the rank of captain. They could not receive the coveted Order of Christ—as Camarão and Henrique Dias had done in the preceding century—but only the less valued Order of Santiago. A royal dispatch of the 29 May 1761 which envisaged the formation of a native clergy for Moçambique[12] remained a

[12] Commenting on the royal decree of 1761, Canon Alcantara Guerieno writes: "Dois séculos quase passaram já sobre este escrito e ainda está para ser ordenado o primeiro sacerdote indígena de Moçambique, apesar de todos os esforços, animados por inúmeros documentos pontifícios, concordantes com este officio régio de D. José I" ('Quadros historicos de Moçambique,' in *Moçambique. Documentario Trimestral*, No. 70, pp. 23-24, 1952). This is, perhaps, not absolutely accurate. One of the sons of the Monomotapa was ordained as a Dominican friar, and he taught theology at Goa *circa* 1658. Alexander Hamilton, writing in 1727, alleged that among the slaves from Moçambique exported to Portuguese India, "some that have the good fortune to be young and docile, and fall into the hands of a zealous superstitious master, are brought up to letters, and in the end come to be priests. I have known many coal-black priests about Goa" (*A new account of the East Indies*, ed. W. Foster, 1930, 2 vols., Vol. I, p. 18). Perhaps Hamilton mistook Kanarese for Negroes; but even if he was correct, the fact remains that these Moçambique Negroes were ordained not in East Africa but in Goa. Many of the priests who served in East Africa, on the other hand, were Goans.

dead letter, although there were many secular clergy of Negro blood in the Portuguese West African possessions. In so far as higher education for laymen was concerned, the Crown in 1704 had ordered that coloured Brazilian students (*pardos*, not full-blooded Negroes) should be admitted to the University of Coimbra, despite the reluctance of the university authorities to do so. As things turned out, very few were able to take advantage of this ruling during the eighteenth century.

As regards the suppression of the Society of Jesus in Portuguese territories—soon to be followed by similar action in Spain and France and ultimately, if temporarily, by the Papacy — the results were almost wholly disastrous. Pombal had a phobia about the Jesuits which can be compared with Ultramontane Catholics' horror of Freemasons, or with anti-Semitic fanatics who believe in the protocols of Zion. Whatever the failings of the Jesuits, the fact remains that they were the best educators, teachers, and missionaries in the Portuguese colonial world. Their sudden and drastic removal left gaps which were not filled for centuries, if indeed they have all been filled at the present day. More especially, Portuguese influence in Asia received a blow from which it never recovered. Their loss was the more severely felt since none of the other Religious Orders nor the secular clergy were capable of replacing them— still less the improvised lay school-teachers on whom Pombal optimistically relied.

I mentioned previously the low standard of the colonial clergy in general, with the exception of the Jesuits and the Capuchins. The reasons given for this state of affairs by contemporaries were as follows. (i) The lax upbringing of boys in slave households, where they were surrounded by half-naked coloured women whom they could enjoy as they pleased. Changing from a lay to an ecclesiastical life, many of them found it impossible to become chaste, and indeed relatively few attempted to do so. (ii) Reluctance to learn the indigenous languages, and hence their dependence on native interpreters and catechists. The Jesuits had always made a point of learning those languages, and in the Maranhão they went so far as to prevent their Amerindian converts from learning Portuguese. (iii) Lack of any real vocation in a great number of priests and friars. It was a common Portuguese practice, explicitly recommended by Dom Francisco Manuel de Mello in his *Guide for Married Men*, that a father should not keep his bastard boys at home, but ship them off to India, or make them take the tonsure.[13] (iv) Insufficiency of clerical stipends in some regions, and the payment of stipends in kind in others, forced many of the clergy to engage in trade in order to maintain themselves.

All things considered, it is hardly surprising that the official correspondence of the period abounds in complaints of lax, simoniacal, and concupiscent clergy. Foreign travellers to Portugal and her overseas possessions during the eighteenth century, whether Roman Catholic or Protestant, are likewise virtually unanimous in their condemnation of the colonial clergy. There were, of course, some exceptions, other than the Jesuits and Capuchins, whom I have already mentioned. An instance of self-sacrificing and successful missionary work was provided by a group of Goan Oratorian priests, whose labours saved the Roman Catholic community of Ceylon from extinction under Dutch rule. Even in Moçambique, where the standards of both secular and Dominican missionaries sank to an exceedingly low level in the second half of the eighteenth century, an official report of 1770 stated that

[13] "A India e a Religião costumão dar boa acolhida a este genero de gente. Sizo será destinarlha", *Carta de guia de casados* (Lisboa, 1651), fl. 125, a popular work which was often reprinted. Cf. also Serafim Leite, *História da Companhia de Jesus no Brasil* (Rio de Janeiro, 1938-50), 10 vols., Vol. 7, pp. 233-47.

there were some honourable exceptions to the general rule. [14]

One thing that Pombal achieved with his suppression of the Society of Jesus, was to break the stranglehold (if that is the right word) of the Church on education. His reform of the University of Coimbra, and his extinction of the Jesuit University of Evora and of the Jesuit colleges overseas, inaugurated a sharp decline in the preponderantly clerical nature of Portuguese culture. Historians differ greatly among themselves as to whether this was, on balance, a good or a bad thing. But whatever we may think of it, this secularization of education was one of the most lasting results of Pombal's reforms, and one which prepared the way for the abolition of the Religious Orders in 1834.

The second half of Pombal's long dictatorship more or less coincided with an acute economic crisis for the Portuguese empire as a whole. Among the factors which caused this crisis was a steady and at times a steep decline in the production of Brazilian gold, diamonds, and sugar. Since the Brazil trade constituted between eighty and ninety per cent of Portugal's colonial commerce, this was a very serious matter. Fortunately for Portugal, things improved during the rule of the (mad) Queen D. Maria I (1777–1792), largely because of Portugal's neutrality in the War of American Independence. This neutrality enabled her colonial trade to revive, at least in part, and to find new European markets for certain Brazilian products such as rice, cotton, and cacao, the cultivation of which had been fostered by Pombal's privileged trading companies.

The American War of Independence naturally caused (or stimulated existing) ideas about freedom in other parts

---

[14] "Isto não é querer persuadir que todos os frades são maus, quando ha, e tem havido, ainda na relaxação das maiores liberdades n'estas terras, individuos de boa moral e costumes" (report of Governor Bernardo Pereira do Lago, Moçambique, 1770, cited in J. de Andrade Corvo, *Estudos sobre as provincias ultramarinas* (Lisboa, 1883-87), 4 vols., Vol. 2, p. 107).

of the New World. Brazil was not immune from this influence, and an abortive plan for proclaiming the independence of the colony was suffocated in Minas Gerais in 1789. This repression proved of little avail, discontent with Portuguese rule being further stimulated by the French Revolution, which had world-wide repercussions. Lord Macartney, the first English ambassador to China, who called at Rio de Janeiro in December 1792 on his way out to Peking, wrote prophetically of the situation as he saw it there:

Rio, if not depressed and smothered by the apprehensive jealousy of Portugal, the parent state, will undoubtedly very soon grow to be a most opulent and flourishing country. But the rising spirit of the people, and the late insurrection at the Mines, together with a sort of prophetic sensation, have so alarmed the Court of Lisbon that they seem determined to distress and starve, instead of nursing and promoting their colonies, and to strangle their children in the cradle, from a dread of their being too strong when they grow up. But it signifies nothing; the Crown of Portugal must either soon transport its seat of empire to Brazil, or leave Brazil to take its own chance by itself. For, in spite of all political or commercial regulations and restrictions, it must soon burst the bud and unfold and exert its native powers, uninfluenced by the weight and unrepressed by the terror of a distant sceptre.[15]

His lordship proved a true if a trifle long-winded prophet. Admittedly, ideas of freedom and independence on the American or on the French model, were for long confined

[15] Macartney's journal, dated the 11 December 1792, as quoted in Helen Robbins, *Our first ambassador to China. An account of the life of George, Earl of Macartney, 1737-1806* (London, 1908), pp. 192-93. An excellent survey of the Brazilian scene on the eve of independence is given by Caio Prado, Junior, *Formação do Brasil contemporâneo. Colônia*, 4 ed. (São Paulo, 1953).

to a small, though influential, circle of educated people; but other factors were at work fermenting the yeast of Brazilian unrest. Brazilians of all classes were resentful of the predominant part played by Portuguese immigrants, who, being generally more energetic than their American-born cousins, virtually monopolized the trade and commerce of the country. The *filhos de Portugal* (sons of Portugal) were also apt to be unduly favoured and protected by their compatriots who comprised the great majority of the government officials. There was also increasing discontent among the free coloured (Mulatto) population against the legal discrimination which was exercised against them in theory, if not always in practice. Finally, there was a general feeling that Portugal could do nothing more for her South American colony, and was not capable of using it other than as a milch-cow of the Portuguese Crown.

The independence of Brazil would not, in any case, have been much longer delayed, as Macartney foresaw in 1792. But it was hastened by Portugal's involvement in the Revolutionary and Napoleonic wars, which led to the flight of the Prince-Regent to Brazil in 1808. This in turn led to the abandonment of the system of colonial monopoly, and the throwing open of Brazil to English trade and to direct foreign influences. The actual break came in 1821-25, but this was merely the belated consummation of a fact recognized as long ago as 1732, when the most experienced Overseas Councillor of the Portuguese Crown advised his royal master as follows:

It is obvious that if Brazil and Portugal[16] are balanced against each other in the scales, the former will weigh

[16] "e bem se deixa ver que, posto em uma balança o Brasil, a na outra o reino, ha de pesar com grande excesso mais aquella que esta; e assim, a maior parte e a mais rica não soffrerá ser dominada pela menor, mais pobre; nem a este inconveniente se lhe poderá achar facil remedio" (*parecer* of António Rodrigues da Costa in the Conselho Ultramarino, Lisboa, 1732, in *Revista do Instituto Histórico e Geográfico Brasileiro*, Tomo VII, 2nd ed. (1866), pp. 498-506).

far more heavily then the latter; and thus the greater and richer part will inevitable refuse to be dominated by the smaller and poorer. Nor is it easy to find a remedy for this situation.

On concluding this rapid survey of the four centuries of Portugal's overseas expansion which began with the conquest of Ceuta in 1415 and ended with the recognition of Brazilian independence in 1825, what sort of a balance-sheet can be struck, and what kind of judgements made? Very different answers are given by historians to these questions, and I will only venture the following tentative and personal reflections.

First, as regards some of the effects on Portugal itself. In the fourteenth and fifteenth centuries, and for the first half of the sixteenth, Portugal drove a brisk trade with northern Europe in her own shipping, and her vessels visited English and Flemish ports. By the end of the sixteenth century, however, all her shipping and all her sailors were needed for the India, Africa and Brazil voyages. Between 1600 and 1800 hardly a single Portuguese ship ventured into the English Channel, and very few into the Mediterranean. Although the Portuguese empire was a sea-borne empire if ever there was one, the mother country did not always have enough sailors and shipping to cope adequately with her own colonial trade, a part of which was sometimes carried in foreign (chiefly English) shipping.

Several seventeenth-century critics and some modern writers assert that Portugal's overseas expansion, and particularly her rickety Eastern empire, brought about the decay of agriculture and industry in the home country, and a decrease in its population. It is alleged that these ills were largely due to excessive emigration, and that the lucky emigrants who eventually did return from the East. brought ostentatious and demoralizing habits with them. which infected society at home. These allegations are either greatly exaggerated or else wholly false. Portugal's population seems to have remained roughly stationery at about 1,200,000 during the period 1540–1640; but in the last quarter of the seventeenth century it began in increase, and numbered about 2,500,000 by the mid-eighteenth century. If, in some regions of Portugal, agriculture and industry decayed in the sixteenth to eighteenth centuries. in other parts they held their own, or even modestly flourished at times. Much of the land was always un-cultivated, and most of the industries were always rudimentary, whether in the Middle Ages or until very recent times.

One benefit which Portugal did derive from her overseas possessions, was that by virtue of them, and the resources which she derived from them, she was able to escape the fate of Scotland and of Catalonia. If "Golden Goa'' eventually turned out to have more glitter than gold, and if the Asian settlements were an economic burden to Portugal since the early seventeenth century (if not before), Brazil, as Dom João IV admitted, was her milch-cow for most of the seventeenth and for all of the eighteenth century. It was successively Brazilian sugar and tobacco, Brazilian gold and diamonds, and finally Brazilian cotton and hides which supplemented Portugal's own modest economy of fruits, wine, and salt. It was also Brazilian sugar, gold and diamonds which secured the interest and hence the support of England in helping to maintain Portuguese independence.

These Brazilian products, in their turn, were only secured by the use of Negro slave labour. It was on the west African slave-trade that Portugal's empire of the South Atlantic

90

depended, not merely for its prosperity but for its existence. Even the independence of Brazil in 1821 did not alter the economic facts of life there for many years. Slavery was only abolished in 1888, and even after that, Brazil continued to be essentially what she had been under Portuguese rule: a producer of primary tropical products—in the late nineteenth century chiefly coffee and rubber—for the European and North American markets, on which her plantation and mining economy was entirely dependent. Only in our own day has she taken a decided step forward with the beginnings of large-scale industrialization.

In tropical Africa, where Portugal was the first European colonizing power, and, if present form is any guide, may soon be the last one left, the proper development of her possessions was thwarted for centuries by the concentration of all efforts on the slave-trade.[17] There were other retarding factors, such as the extreme unhealthiness of many regions, like the Zambezi river valley, which made white colonization impossible before the discoveries of modern science provided antidotes against malaria and other tropical diseases. But it was the slave-trade with its demoralizing results for both slaver and enslaved which formed the greatest handicap and which left the largest liability, both in Africa and in Brazil. *Trabalho é para cachorro e Negro*, "Work is for a cur and a Nigger", as the Brazilian saying goes.

Cf. Bento Banha Cardoso, one of the *conquistadores* of Angol.., in his account of the natural resources of that kingdom in 1622: "de todas estas cousas se fez lá mui pouco caso, porque empregados os homens commummente no resgate dos negros se descuidam do mais" (*apud* Luciano Cordeiro, *Viagens, explorações e conquistas dos Portugueses, 1620-1629. Producções, comercio e governo do Congo e Angola* (Lisboa 1881), p. 18): "Emquanto se occupavam todos em fazer do Negro uma mercadoria, não podia ninguem cuidar, com energia a perseverança, de cultivar a terra, e tirar proveito da feracidade do solo e das muitas e importantes riquezas que alli ha" (João de Andrade Corvo, *Estudos sobre as provincias ultramarinas*, Vol. I, 1883, p. 150). It would be easy to multiply such quotations between 1622 and 1883.

The centuries-old Iberian horror of manual labour was reinforced and solidified by a white (or part-white) colonial society which confessedly depended on the Negro slaves for its hands and its feet.

In Brazil, Asia, and Africa, the Portuguese played a useful role in transplanting tropical fruits and vegetables from one continent to another: oranges, pineapples, maize, manioc and tobacco being a few of many instances which could be quoted. More important, some people may think, was the spread of their language and of their religion, which in many places struck deep roots. The Calvinist Scots interloper, Alexander Hamilton, no great admirer of the Portuguese, but a man who knew the countries bordering on the Indian Ocean like the back of his hand, wrote in 1727 that he could not find one Asian in ten thousand who spoke English, but plenty who spoke a form of Portuguese.

Along the sea coasts, the Portuguese have left a vestige of their language, tho' much corrupted, yet it is the language that most Europeans learn first, to qualify them for a general converse with one another, as well as with the different inhabitants of India.

At the dawn of the nineteenth century another Scot with great experience of the Eastern seas, wrote to a young friend going out there:

Acquire the native language, both Moors [=Malay] and Portuguese if possible. You will find them of infinite use hereafter.[18]

Many Portuguese words are still embedded in Asian vernaculars, and I have alluded previously to the Roman

[18] Alexander Hamilton, *A New Account of the East Indies*, 1727 (London, 1930), Vol. 1, pp. 7-8; *A narrative of the early life and services of Captain Macdonald, I.N.*, p. 300).

Catholic communities which have survived until our own day. In short, it may be said that the Portuguese chronicler, João de Barros, was not far wrong when he wrote prophetically in 1540:

The Portuguese arms and pillars placed in Africa and in Asia, and in countless isles beyond the bounds of three continents, are material things, and time may destroy them. But time will not destroy the religion, customs, and language which the Portuguese have implanted in those lands.[19]

[19] João de Barros, *Diálogo em louvor da nossa lingua* (Lisboa, 1540).

BIBLIOGRAPHICAL NOTE

Since the titles of all works cited in the footnotes are quoted in full when first mentioned, and their respective authors appear in the index, this list is limited to some of the more important and better documented publications, including several which have appeared since the standard bibliographies of G. Schurhammer S.J. (*Die Zeitgenössischen quellen zur geschichte Portugiesisch-Asiens und zeiner nachbarländer zur zeit des He. Franz Zavier 1538-1552*, Leipzig, 1932) and W. Berriman and R. Borba de Morais (*Manual bibliográfico de estudos brasileiros*, Rio de Janeiro, 1949). It also serves as a guide to further reading for those who wish to deepen as well as widen their knowledge of the subject.

Archivo Portuguez Oriental. Nova Goa, 1857-76. 8 Vols.
> This invaluable publication edited by J. H. da Cunha Rivara should not be confused with its namesake mentioned below. Particularly rich in 16th-18th century documents on Portuguese India.

Arquivo Português Oriental, Nova edição. Bastorá Goa, 1936-40. 11 Vols.
> Edited (very carelessly) by A. B. de Bragança Pereira, and riddled with misreadings and misprints, this series nevertheless contains many interesting documents, which were not included in Cunha Rivara's work. It contains the first integral printing of António Bocarro's *Livro do Estado da India Oriental* compiled in 1634-35.

Arquivo das Colonias. Publicação official e mensal. Lisboa, 1917-31. 5 Vols.
> Contains a wide range of 17th-18th century documents, particularly for the Portuguese possessions in West and East Africa.

AXELSON, ERIC: *Portuguese in South-East Africa. 1600-1700*. Johannesburg, 1960.
> Published after the present work had gone to press, this book advantageously replaces the highly unreliable works of the late S. R. Welch on the same period.

BARROS, JOÃO DE: *Decadas da Asia*. 1552-1615.
> The first three *Decadas* were published at Lisbon during the lifetime of Barros' in 1552, 1553 and 1563, respectively, the fourth being edited in 1615 by João Baptista Lavanha from the notes left by the chronicler. Also available in later editions, of which the most recent is by H. Cidade and M. Murias. Lisboa, 1945-46. 4 Vols.

BOTELHO DE SOUSA, ALFREDO: *Subsídios para a história militar marítima da India, 1585-1669*. Lisboa, 1930-56. 4 Vols.
> Unfortunately the author's death shortly after the publication of the fourth volume, which brings the story down to 1650, prevented the conclusion of this work. Particularly valuable for the war with the Dutch, as the author uses printed Dutch and English as well as Portuguese archival sources.

94

BRÁSIO, ANTÓNIO C. S. Sp.: *Monumenta Missionaria Africana, Africa Ocidental.* Lisboa, 1952—in progress.

The ten volumes published at the time of writing cover the period 1342-1646, and include material from foreign as well as from Portuguese archives.

CADORNEGA, ANTÓNIO DE OLIVEIRA DE: *História Geral das Guerras Angolanas.* Lisboa, 1940-42. 3 Vols.

Written originally at Luanda in 1681-83, the first two volumes were edited by José Matias Delgado and the third, which is in the nature of a geographic and ethnographic survey, by Manuel Alves da Cunha.

CALMON, PEDRO: *História do Brasil, 1500-1800.* São Paulo and Rio de Janeiro, 1939-40. 3 Vols.

Another edition was published in 1959 but it is virtually a reprint of this one which gives a better balanced survey of Brazilian colonial history than F. A. Varnhagen's still useful *História Geral do Brasil antes da sua separação e independencia de Portugal,* 4th ed. São Paulo, 1948-49. 5 Vols.

Cartas de Affonso de Albuquerque seguidas de documentos que as elucidam. Lisboa, 1884-1935. 7 Vols.

Edited by R. A. de Bulhão Pato and H. Lopes de Mendonça for the Lisbon Academy of Sciences. An unrivalled source for the establishment of the Portuguese thalassocracy in the Indian Ocean.

Cartas de Dom João de Castro. Lisboa, 1954.

Edited by Elaine Sanceau, these most interesting letters by one of the greatest figures of Portuguese Asia cover the decade 1539-48.

CORTESÃO, JAIME: *Alexandre de Gusmão e o tratado de Madrid.* Rio de Janeiro, 1950-59. 8 Vols.

An excellent and lavishly documented work which is indispensable for the study of 18th-century Brazil.

COUTO, DIOGO DO: *Decadas da Asia.* Lisboa, 1602-1788.

References to *Decadas* VI-VIII and *Decada* XII are from the original 17th-century editions of 1602-1673, and those to the other *Decadas* are taken from the collected edition of 14 vols., Lisboa, 1778-88. Couto lived for over fifty years in Portuguese India and his work will always be indispensable for a study of its history, the seamy side of which is exposed in his *O soldado prático,* ed. M. Rodrigues Lapa. Lisboa, 1937.

DELGADO, RALPH. *História de Angola, 1482-1836.* Benguela and Lobito, 1948-55. 4 Vols.

The four volumes published so far cover the period 1482-1737, and are based principally on the documents in the Arquivo Histórico Ultramarino, Lisboa.

LEITE, SERAFIM S. J.: *História da Companhia de Jesus no Brasil.* Lisboa and Rio de Janeiro, 1938-50. 10 Vols.; and *Artes e ofícios dos Jesuitas no Brasil, 1549-1760.* Lisboa, 1953.
Taken together, these 11 volumes form the definitive history of the Jesuits in colonial Brazil, based as they are on a wealth of manuscript and printed sources.

LOBATO, ALEXANDRE: *A Expansão Portuguesa em Moçambique de 1498 à 1530.* Lisboa, 1954-1960. 3 Vols.
It is much to be hoped that the author will continue this richly documented publication, which supersedes all that has been written on the same subject previously.

— — *Evolução administrativa e económica de Moçambique, 1752-1763. Fundamentos da criação do governo geral em 1752.* Lisboa, 1957.
Another excellent work by the same author which deserves continuation.

Moçambique. Documentário Trimestral. Lourenço Marques, 1935-59. 96 Nos.
Contains many well-documented articles by Caetano Montez, Canon Alcantara Guerreiro, and other Moçambique scholars. Now replaced by the *Boletim da Sociedade de Estudos de Moçambique.* Lourenço Marques, 1931 to date.

PISSURLENCAR, PANDURONGA: *Assentos do Conselho do Estado da India, 1618-1750.* Bastorá—Goa, 1953-57. 5 Vols.
An excellent publication by the Chief Archivist at Goa. Particularly valuable for the years 1618-1700.

SÁ, ARTUR DE, *Documentação para a história das missões do padroado português do Oriente. Insulíndia.* Lisboa, 1954—in progress.
The five volumes published to date cover the period 1506-1595, and include a reprint of the very rare *Relações summarias de alguns serviços que fizerão os religiosos Dominicos nas partes da India Oriental.* Lisboa, 1635.

SILVA REGO, ANTÓNIO DA: *Documentação para a história das missões do padroado português do Oriente. India.* Lisboa, 1947—in progress.
The 12 volumes published to date cover the period 1499-1582, and include many documents of more than purely a missionary interest.

STUDIA. REVISTA SEMESTRAL. Lisboa, 1958 to date.
Though no indication is given in the title, this historical magazine is devoted to the history of Portugal's overseas possessions and contains many interesting documents. Edited by Padre António da Silva Rego, Director of the Centro de Estudos Históricos Ultramarinos, Lisboa.

INDEX

Abyssinia 7, 12, 18, 36, 37
Açores 5, 8, 10–12, *passim*
Affonso I (King of Congo) 28–29
Albuquerque, Affonso de
 14–15, 20n, 34, 36, 59
Alcaçer-Kebir, battle of 23
Almeida, Francisco de 15
Alvares, Francisco de 36n
Ambaca 32
Amboina 40, 49, 63
Amerindians, and forced labour
 67–69, 71–72
 Pombal and the freedom of
 83
Anchieta, Joseph de (Jesuit) 30n
Angola, Portuguese in 29–32,
 50–51, 56, 69, 79
 Jesuits in 30, 67
 Dutch in 50–51
Annam 40
Antonil (pseudonym of Jesuit
 Andreoni) 69n, 74n, 78n
Arabs, in the Iberian peninsula
 3–4
 in Indian Ocean 13–16,
 32–35, 37
 see also Oman, Muslims,
 Moors
Arakan, 57
Arguim 24
Axelson, Eric 9n, 34n, 94
Axim 28
Azevedo, Carlos de 15n
Azores *see* Açores

Bahia (Brazil) 71–78 *passim*
Barbosa, Duarte 17
Barbinais, Le Gentil de la 78n
Barros, João de 32, 93, 94
 his account of Guinea 26–28
Batavia 57, 63
Benguela 29, 50, 71, 77
Bijapur 14
Blake, J. W. 25n
Bombay 53
Botelho de Sousa, Alfredo 50n,
 94
Bourbon, island of 79
Bourdonnais, Mahé de la 79

Bovill, E. W. 6n
Braganza, Catarina de 52–53
Brásio, António (C.S.Sp.) 28n,
 30n, 65n, 95
Brazil, early colonization of 18,
 20, 21, 69, 70
 war with the Dutch invaders
 of 51–52, 55, 56
 frontier expansion 71–72, 78–
 79
 gold rush in 73–76
 slave-trade with west Africa
 71, 77–78
 miscegenation in 77–78
 Pombal's policy in 80–86
 passim
 growth of national feeling in
 87–89
 chartered trading companies
 for 82
 as milch-cow of Portugal 70,
 88, 90
 see also Amerindians, Sugar,
 Slaves
Buddhists and Buddhism,
 Portuguese attitude to 38, 40

Cadornega, António de Oliveira
 de 31–32, 95
Calado, Manuel (Friar) 62
Calicut 13, 14, 39
Calmon, Pedro 95
Calvinists, unsuccessful in com-
 petition with the Romanists
 63
Camarão 52n, 83
Cambambe 51
Cano, Sebastian del 17
Canton 37, 41
Cardoso, Bento Banha 91n
Cape Delgado 15
Cape Nun 10, 11
Cape Verde Islands 11, 24, 25
Capuchin Friars 84, 85
Cartaz(es) 16
Castello-Novo, Marquis of 79
Ceuta 5, 6, 14, 23, 89
Ceylon 39–40, 63, 85–86
Chappoulie, H. 66n

98

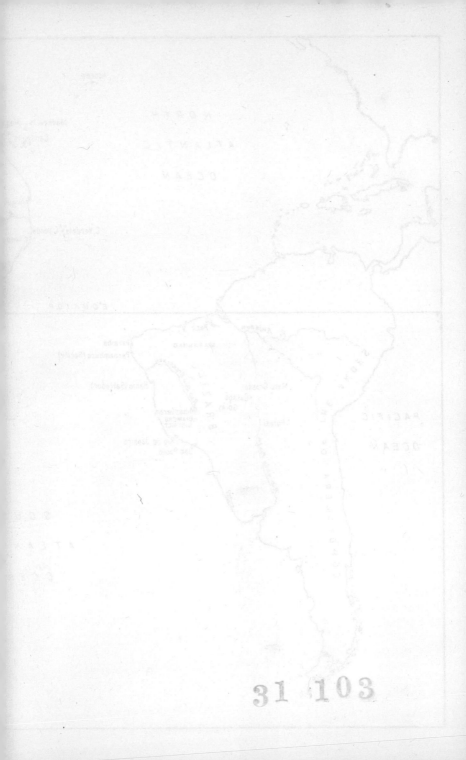

31 103